ON TRYING TO BE HUMAN

'I have got rid of the bribe of bread. I have got rid of the bribe of Heaven. Let God's work be done for its own sake: the work he had to create us to do because it cannot be done except by living men and women.'

Shaw (*Major Barbara*)

ON TRYING
TO BE
HUMAN

ROSEMARY HAUGHTON

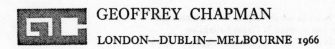
GEOFFREY CHAPMAN
LONDON—DUBLIN—MELBOURNE 1966

Geoffrey Chapman Ltd.,
18 High Street, Wimbledon, London S.W.19

Geoffrey Chapman (Ireland) Ltd.,
5–7 Main Street, Blackrock, Co. Dublin, Ireland

Geoffrey Chapman Pty. Ltd.,
459 Little Collins Street, Melbourne, Australia

This book is set in Imprint 101 11 on 13pt
Made and printed in Great Britain by
Blackie and Son Ltd., Bishopbriggs, Glasgow

CONTENTS

This book is dedicated with gratitude to the person who provoked me into attempting to weave many ideas into one garland—

ἵνα φθαρτὸν στέφανον λάβωσιν, ἡμεῖς δὲ ἄφθαρτον

PREFACE

When Mrs Haughton told me of her plan for this book, I knew that she was going to give us a work of unusual value. I was not mistaken. But now that I have read it, read it twice in fact, and am faced with the task of writing a few introductory words, I hardly know what to say except: read it. She is a writer of astonishing originality. Her thoughts are always her own, and she uses language in a fresh, personal way that avoids all the tired phrases common in most religious writing. I feel reluctant to interpose my own more standardized thinking between her and the reader. However, since she has honoured me with an invitation to do so, I will attempt a few remarks.

People often forget that the Christian message is offered as an interpretation of human experience and an answer to the problem of human living. What Christians call the gift of grace is present universally. Man left to his own resources, man untouched by God's grace, is a non-existent abstraction. It should therefore be possible to take the concrete experience of actual men and find pointers to the Christian interpretation, features that are illuminated and made meaningful by the Gospel teaching. And Christians struggling to make sense of their own lives in the light of the Gospel should be able to discover much common ground with all those who are trying to be human, trying to follow out all the implications they discern in their humanity when they search for human wholeness. Mrs Haughton has taken up this double possibility. She has tried to understand the direction and meaning of human experience and, in doing so, to relate it to Christ's teaching. Her hope is that the attempt, while helping Christians, will also help those who are not Christians to understand Christianity better and recognize a common effort to become fully human.

The book, I think, succeeds admirably in its purpose. Despite a difficult beginning, the reader is soon held by the account of human development as the author takes him through its stages: the desire for freedom, the initial commitment to search for it, the sound relationships which condition the successful beginning of development, the breakthrough of the spirit by passionate response in relation, the extension of self-discovery in the wider relation of community, the healthy acceptance of the dark, untameable area of unconscious life, the use of suffering for the release of the spirit. But I must not summarize. Mrs Haughton will speak best for herself. I should simply like to point to her brilliant and authentic use of the Pauline distinction between flesh and spirit, the enlightening way she develops and handles the concept of passion, and her understanding of the symbolic function of sex.

A strong reason for welcoming the book is that it will serve to meet a great weakness in the present work of Christian renewal. Many people, including myself, are uncomfortably aware that the stream of ideas, suggestions and changes now pouring forth is passing by and leaving unaffected most ordinary Christians, let alone those who are not Christians. I think that the weakness I refer to is probably best illustrated by the young people who are still leaving the Church in great numbers and who, when articulate, confess that the faith has become quite meaningless to them. They cannot link the faith with their experience, an experience which, though puzzling, is often in them so intense and so absorbing. There has in fact been a failure to relate the riches of recent Christian thinking to ordinary human experience. The lofty, remote and self-contained isolation of professional Christian writing troubles even those already familiar with the jargon. If Christian renewal is not to remain a theological and institutional tidying-up, it must begin to ask questions about the fundamental experience of men as they struggle in their living towards human fulfilment. Men today are conscious of themselves as free subjects responsible for their own development. Many have thrown off allegiance to the Christian Church to liberate themselves from a seeming ecclesiastical refusal to allow men to grow and be themselves. They need to be shown again that the Christian faith is concerned with the conditions for the achievement of a human wholeness in freedom. This book is an attempt to do that.

I found the book personally very helpful. Others, I am sure, will find the same. Convinced of its easily recognizable value, I am not afraid to express some reservations about it. Mrs Haughton herself, I know, would not want me to indulge an uncritical enthusiasm.

It is a ruthlessly honest book. Part of its honesty is indeed the recognition that complete honesty is impossible. But it is as personally honest as Mrs Haughton can make it. Now, such personal honesty has its weakness as well as its undoubted strength. The weakness is the tendency to reduce the entire Christian tradition to what happens to be personally relevant here and now. When honesty means the dominance of personal reference as a criterion of truth, then the content of Christian tradition is accepted in so far as it is personally meaningful and personally liberating. Ultimately, however, this makes one a prisoner of a limited experience. Let me take an example from literary tradition. It would prevent a possible change or development of sensibility, were one to refuse to preserve and hand on that literature of the past which was no longer congenial to our present taste or meaningful in our present circumstances. What does not speak to our generation may well become a living voice to the next. Fortunately, the great tradition of Christian teaching and the thought of the great masters of Christian theology and spirituality have been handed down to us by generations faithful to authority when much in what they passed on was not to them personally very meaningful. What would, for example, have happened to the liturgy if past generations had omitted all that did not correspond to the personal outlook of their time? The Christian tradition is in fact supported by an external authority with objective criteria for its application. Such authority would be meaningless, unless received with a free, personal acceptance.

But once received, it judges our personal experience and insights; it is not judged by them. The Christian tradition as an external norm is an educative support for our personal development. But it is more than that. It is a sign of what lies beyond our power of personal assimilation, what reveals the limits of our present experience, what will not be surpassed until the reality it manifests is directly grasped.

Mrs Haughton has not set out to give a comprehensive account of Christian teaching, and it would be wrong to judge her book as if that were her purpose. She has, as I know from herself, deliberately limited her scope in order to discover how far an honest examination of common human experience would take one towards the Christian faith. The limits of the book are not for herself the limits of Christianity. I should have liked, however, more manifest and operative in the book itself the conviction that the interpretative appropriation of personal development she describes takes place for the Christian under the guidance of the Christian tradition and does not stand above it as its judge. There is more in the New Testament itself than she has accounted for. That she would readily admit, but she does not clearly say so.

I do not want these hesitations of an unrepentant theologian to obscure the value of this remarkable book. Rather, may they by pointing to its limits encourage others who may be more hesitant than myself confidently to assimilate its positive contribution. This provides an enrichment we badly need.

CHARLES DAVIS

INTRODUCTION

ALL the advances in knowledge that have been made in the last century (though their roots go much further back than that) have combined to form a huge question mark. The question is not a new one, in fact it is as old as human thought. What is a human being? That is what humans begin to ask as soon as the basic necessities of existence have been satisfied. What is new is that the old answers have been called in question so generally that whereas dissatisfaction with traditional answers was formerly confined to the minority of the educated, it is now becoming the usual thing. But there is another element which is new. This is the fact that many people, in answer to the challenge of new knowledge, try to express a new and deeper and more homogeneous understanding of the human condition and destiny in ways and words that are old, and that formerly were generally held to express more limited concepts. (Although there have always been those who saw further than the ends of their own words, they have been exceptional and usually misunderstood.) These people, who are Christian believers, naturally use the same vocabulary as many who still understand the world as their forefathers did and who accept the old answers in the old categories to the perennial question; but they are beginning to wonder what the old and new expressions really have in common beyond a traditional vocabulary.

On the other hand there are many who, finding themselves forced to reject the old answers, labour to achieve a new understanding in this largely uncharted field of living, driven by the desire for truth that will not let a man rest once he has allowed himself to recognise its existence in himself. These are the unbelievers; the real ones, as opposed to those who are too cowardly or too lazy or too stupid (or just too busy doing something else) to believe or unbelieve anything, whose opinions are all second-hand and involve no personal search or commitment.

The tragedy is that when many Christians and unbelievers are simultaneously struggling to discover the meaning of a human life whose range of knowledge has suddenly become so much vaster and whose nature is seen to be so much more problematic than ever before, their efforts, instead of bringing them together, push them apart.

Both realise in themselves the call they cannot in conscience ignore, the call to become human. They have become aware of the challenge of possibly risky discovery, of commitment to the unknown, yet they, a minority on whom so much depends, are divided on either side of a great gulf. The gulf cannot be crossed from one side only—the foundations at least of the bridge must be laid on each side. This book does not, therefore, attempt to build a whole bridge.

What I have tried to do in this book is to examine the experience of human life and see if and how Christianity illuminates the search for the fullness of being human. Christianity claims both to assist the understanding of what it means to be human and to show the way to achieve man's proper destiny. In examining this claim in relation to experiences which are common to all I write, necessarily, as a Christian, in the hope that my attempts to discover what it means to be a human being will help other Christians, and that those who are not Christians will, as it were, read over my shoulder and gain some insight into the experience of life as Christianity conceives it. I have tried to take nothing for granted, and to be as honest as possible in examining the evidence both for and against the Christian approach. Complete honesty I do not claim, because it is not possible to be entirely honest (this radical difficulty in human living is discussed in one chapter of this book). But the desire for truth is the motive of this book, since only a willingness to search and a refusal to turn back from even the most uncomfortable implications of one's discoveries is implicit in writing such a book at all. This willingness to search is therefore one of the things discussed in the book.

If the gap between believer and unbeliever cannot be crossed by the believer alone, there is one gap that can and must be crossed before the search for full humanity can even begin, and that is the one within the Christian mind itself between the believer and the hidden unbeliever, whose very existence many of us are unwilling to acknowledge. He is thought of as a potential traitor, a menace to faith and peace of mind. He should, on the contrary, be welcomed as an ally and a means of understanding the difficulties of other people.

Criticism of a faith is a personal attack only if the indwelling unbeliever is really an enemy, waiting to sell the pass. But if a Christian can find in himself sufficient humility to throw away natural resentment (and no one more than the Christian should realise that this is a necessary struggle) then the indwelling doubter may become a mediator, and criticism cease to be an attack and become a bridge, a means of communication. Therefore in introducing this book it is worth while to examine the strength of this bridge. Is there a real link between faith and experience? Which comes first and what is the relationship?

Most people do not come to any kind of religious faith by way of an analysis of the human condition and its needs, and of the possible extra-human significance of those needs. The process of religious commitment, whether it comes about by a definite and dateable 'conversion' or by evolution through childhood teaching to a more mature understanding and acceptance, takes place mostly below the conscious level, and it is usually expressed in language which is traditional, or has no significance for the non-believer. This initial failure of communication comes about because the words used are, for the unbeliever, linked to realities in himself of which he is not consciously aware but which are, as it were, brought into operation by the overtones (echoing in himself) of the traditional words and phrases. The realities to which the words are intended to refer are not a Christian monopoly, but Christianity has identified and explained and labelled them in a coherent way which makes them available as ideas to ordinary people. This is why words like 'salvation', 'repentance' or even 'God', which puzzle or revolt or infuriate the unbeliever, can be used without intellectual discomfort by believers who are every bit as intelligent, honest and self-critical as their unbelieving friends. But it is hard to the point of impossibility for the unbeliever to accept this, and when he tries to explain to himself the paradox of his believing friends' combination of faith with honest intelligence he is forced to think up some such hypothesis as that the believer's unconscious needs oblige him to seek the support of a religious system. Therefore, he supposes, the believer keeps this necessary faith in a separate compartment of his mind, labelled 'supernatural', where it cannot be touched by the operations of reason. In other words, religion appears to the unbeliever as a sort of diseased growth on the otherwise healthy psychological condition of the believer, even though the experiences to which religious words refer may in fact be identical with experiences of his own.

The believer, on his side, is conscious of no such separation. He uses the traditional words and is unaware, or only vaguely aware, of how much larger are the 'things' to which he is referring than his words can possibly be expected to indicate to the non-believer. Nor does he generally realise—and this is the crucial point—what are the points of contact, if any, between his 'religious' concepts and the experiences of human life which are common to all men. He is distressed and baffled by the obvious discomfort of his unbelieving friends when he talks about what he believes. He tries to explain, using the only words he knows, and what he says sounds to his friends and often to himself a horrible jumble of primitive magic, evasion of reality and unconscious self-deception. The result is no rapprochement but a deepening gulf which may become so deep and wide that contact becomes impossible. And this is disastrous for both sides, because the thing that matters most of all in human life is the ability to communicate. To the unbeliever religion is itself the obstacle to communication, one which needs to be removed. He cannot see that to 'remove' religion would be to destroy the very things about which he wants to find common ground, because the roots of religious ideas spread right through human life, and the little shoot above ground is only a small part of them. The believer, on the other hand, very often sees the problem in the same way, and wants to remove the obstacles of unbelief by showing how reasonable is his faith. He only makes matters worse, because he is making the same mistake. The mental and spiritual processes by which a human being grapples with the realities of his existence and comes to terms with them (if he does) are continuous and organic. The words by which he expresses them are symbols labelling certain little shoots that, as it were, project above the surface and require to be identified before further progress is possible, for the process is simultaneously 'above' and 'below' the surface. The believer's attempts at 'explanation' are necessarily confined to the area 'above' the surface, and when he refers to what is 'below' he uses apparently arbitrary symbols which, as I said, mean something to him for reasons he does not normally recognise. He is, therefore, using these symbols as if they referred to conscious and acknowledged and identified experiences.

The failure of communication is not confined to verbal misunderstandings, fundamental though these may be in their effects. Failure in communication is basically the cause of most man-made human ills, and in a wider sense perhaps it is at the root of 'natural' ills as well. Failure in communication prevents people tackling energetically, for instance, the problem of world hunger. The response that the need of another might evoke is blocked by the fear of uncovering one's own vulnerable spots, politically or individually. If I begin to give, where will it end? If I admit my responsibility in some degree, shall I not be forced to go much further than will be comfortable for me? And if, by doing so, I lose something of my financial prestige, will not others take advantage of me? The politician, for instance, may privately think it right to devote a large part of the national income to nations who are in need. He dare not say so, because he thinks the electorate will not follow him in his desire to help, and he would not then be re-elected. This would expose him, personally, to insecurity, and he would lose such influence as he might hope to use for good. Nor can he rely on help in his own need. He feels the threat of an isolation which may not hurt too much as long as one's material security is assured, but which becomes terrifying when this is threatened. So, in self-defence, we refuse to respond to the needs of others, we refuse to receive this 'communication' of need or, on our side, to 'communicate' by sympathy, because that would mean letting down our defences. This is only one limited example of the way people find themselves afraid, which in practice means unable, to communicate, and I have used it to show that I am using the word 'communicate' in the wide sense of a real contact between people, whether direct or not, verbally expressed or not. In the failure to communicate there is always the element of fear, the fear of exposing oneself not merely to the other person, but primarily to oneself. This is why attempts to rouse people to action, either 'charitable' action or aggressive action (as in wartime), must rely on the creation of artificial emotional reactions of the appropriate type, strong enough to overcome the fear of self-exposure.

So the failure of communication seems to be between man and man but also fundamentally within human nature itself. We not only do not understand ourselves, we are afraid to do so. Each human being is 'enclosed', cut off not only from other human beings but from the greater part of his own self. Saying this does not necessarily mean accepting the findings of any particular school of depth psychology. It is simply a way of saying that there is a terrifying amount that we don't know about how human beings function, physically and psychologically, and more particularly that we are largely ignorant of the links between these two aspects of human life.

Yet it would be arbitrary at this stage to describe this 'enclosed' or 'limited' condition as 'wrong', since we have no experience of any other, and therefore, it would seem, no standard by which to measure 'rightness' or 'wrongness' in this connection. On the other hand we certainly know more than we used to about the

workings of the human body and mind, and most people regard
this as an 'improvement' in the human condition, unless they are
frightened by the implications of this knowledge in presenting
choices of a dangerous kind which were not formerly possible. It
seems likely, for instance, that research may lead to the possibility,
in the forseeable future, of the manipulation of the human mind
to produce behaviour planned by the manipulator. This is a
drastic advance on the technique known as 'brain washing', but
points in the same direction. The possibilities inherent in this
are so horrifying that many would prevent, forcibly if necessary,
the type of increase of knowledge that leads to the wielding of
such dangerous power. Still, the fear of this kind of increase in
knowledge is not so much a contradiction of the idea that its
increase (or, to put it another way, the pushing back of the walls
of the 'enclosure') is 'right', as a comparison with another and
perhaps more fundamental kind of 'rightness'—the increased
power to make the 'right' moral decisions. The fear is that moral
sensibility has not kept pace with the advance of physical knowledge, and that such knowledge will therefore be misused—again
a value judgment. The power to make 'right' moral decisions
itself implies 'knowledge', the knowledge of long-term purposes
for human living, the 'right' purposes. So wherever we look we
find the assumption that there is a 'right' and a 'wrong' way to
use human nature, and that therefore it is 'right' to advance in
knowledge because this makes us more likely to use human
nature 'rightly'. Doubts about the rightness of advances in
knowledge are always due to the fear that it is, in fact, not whole
knowledge but one-sided and therefore misleading. (In fact
it is impossible even to say this without implying the same kind of
moral judgment. I said 'whole' knowledge, implying some standard
of 'wholeness' by which other kinds of knowledge are judged to be
incomplete and therefore *mis*leading.) In practice we assume that
the human condition is imperfect, and not only can but should be
improved. This 'improvement' is the movement towards a more
complete discovery of what it means to be human.

But there is more to it than this, without moving out of the realm of experience. We do not assume merely that it is right and possible to improve the human condition 'quantitatively', by gradually increasing understanding of ourselves and each other and applying the results of increased knowledge to the service of human happiness. As far back as written records will take us, as much further back as myths and folk-tales and archaeological bits and pieces can give grounds for well-supported guesses, there has been a desire to break right out of the human condition as we know it, in its enclosed state, and enter upon another kind of existence altogether. There is not only a desire to do this but a conviction that it can be done, and this despite the fact that every actual, recorded attempt to do so has ended, as far as we can see, in a return to the normal, enclosed condition of human living. Some people, it is true, have claimed to have passed into this 'other' existence and thereafter to have been in continuous contact with it. Many great religious leaders, including Christ, have made this claim, and it was the fascination of the claim that gave their doctrine its powerful appeal. Besides figures obviously worthy of reverence, there have been less reputable ones who made the same claim, notably members of the movement of the 'Free Spirit' in the middle ages and, later, the Ranters in England. Some have believed their claim, some have not. We are not in a position to verify from our own experience or study a claim which relates to things which are, by their very nature, beyond the reach of sensory experience or intellectual definition. But it is not the very few who claim to have succeeded in entering another kind of existence who are interesting in this connection, and whether their claim is true or false, it is irrelevant to the discussion at this point. What is interesting is the desire for this 'escape' among ordinary people, and the persistence of the belief in its possibility.

This persistence is, on the whole, racial rather than personal. Many individuals, especially as they get older, give up hoping for 'a way out' and turn their minds deliberately to the things they can reasonably hope to secure—financial and physical security, family affection, or the betterment of the human lot in the 'quantitative' or 'horizontal' sense. Sometimes their personal abandonment of the quest for a 'way out' leads them to condemn violently the hopes of others who are still searching. This violence shows, in itself, how strong is the drive to freedom that requires such a display of scorn in order to reassure the 'realist' that he is right to reject the search as illusory and to assume the absolute non-existence of what cannot be verified by the senses. But whatever the individual may do this desire will not be suppressed. The young usually feel it most strongly, but many, and not only those who are obviously poets or mystics, keep it all their lives and gradually refine away their earlier, cruder suppositions (which are often not even stated but only acted on) about how this liberation might be achieved.

In the past this drive towards freedom has generally been interpreted in a religious sense, but it does not follow that everyone who believed a particular religion understood its teachings as relating to his personal desire to 'escape' (if he ever put it to himself in such terms, which is not very likely). A system of belief can generally be just as well related to the limited and normally attainable desires of everyday living and this is how many people will always interpret it, using its symbols as magical means of obtaining temporal blessings. On the other hand the practices of religion could and did provide an outlet of a kind for the desire to escape, and could and did support the conviction that escape was possible, if only in the sense that contact was possible between mortal man and beings of a higher and freer kind, whether these were the gods of Olympus or the spirits of the jungle. At certain times, especially times of social unrest and distress, the desire for escape is naturally likely to be at its strongest. It expresses itself in such things as the mystery cults of Egypt, Greece and Rome, the cult of witchcraft, all kinds of magic and satanism, and sects with a heavy emphasis on mystical experiences, such as flourish among the descendants of African slaves in the West Indies.

This is not a study in comparative religion. The different levels and methods of liberation proposed by different faiths are fascinating but not immediately relevant. But it should be

noticed that abandonment of belief in a particular religion, or
any religion, does not, as might be expected and as some of the
earlier depth-psychologists hoped, remove the desire for, or the
obstinate hope of, a way of escape from the human condition of
enclosure. The methods tried by many people now are not new,
but in the past these methods were often to be found employed
in a 'religious' attempt to break out, for which they are not,
normally, considered suitable nowadays. Sex, dancing, drugs, even
physical pain—inflicted or suffered—have all been employed in
religious rites for this purpose (and in some small sects they still
are) nor is it new to find them used, for the same though often
unacknowledged purpose, by those who reject religion. What was,
or is, the indulgence in 'orgies' of one kind or another but a search
for a way of escape from the normal condition of life? The fact
that in the past it has usually been the comparatively well-off
who have been able to explore such methods of achieving a
sense of unreality, losing contact more or less completely with the
sense of 'normal' living, is not just a question of money. The rich
were those whose education made an intellectual evaluation (and
consequent rejection) of popular religion possible, but on whom
the necessities of keeping alive did not press physically and
mentally as they did on the poor. Therefore their minds were
free to grapple with the meaning of existence and the apparent
futility of human effort. Whether they thought it out intellectually
or merely reacted emotionally, the result was usually the same—
a reaching for any means to get into a state of mind in which the
essential narrowness, dullness and general idiocy of being human
could be forgotten, a state of mind which, if only temporarily, gave
an experience of freedom and purpose. This can be thought of as
an escape *from*, as in 'excesses' of sex, drink or drugs; or as an
escape *to*, as in the use of vision-inducing drugs by Huxley and
others, in the more 'ordinary' kind of mysticism, or in the ritual
use of sexuality. The aim in both cases is the same.

Nowadays the means of achieving a temporary sensation of
freedom are not, in our civilisation, confined to the rich; or,
rather, 'the rich', at least as compared to the living standards of

their immediate fore-fathers, are vastly more numerous. Hence the wailing over the declining morals of teenagers that can now be heard on all sides. But these young men and women are only doing what human beings have always done, which is to look for a way out of the human condition as they know it. The plumber's apprentice and other young people quoted in *Generation X* who 'live for kicks', the Roman aristocrat at one of Nero's curious dinner parties, the dervish whirling himself into ecstasy, or the Buddhist monk seeking enlightenment by detachment from desire are all on the same quest, though not by any means all at the same stage.

But the fact that, as far back as we can probe, human beings have desired freedom from the normal human condition of enclosure does not imply that the condition can be altered, or even that there are any objective grounds for the feeling that it 'should' be different. Whether the 'feeling' corresponds to some reality or whether it be a compensation (for what?) a 'drive' (towards what?), a carrot for the donkey (who holds the carrot?) or just a disease, we cannot judge on the evidence of the thing itself. We can only know that this is how the human condition 'feels', and, in an attempt to discover what may be meant by the fullness or completeness of human life, this 'feeling' must be given the large place it does actually occupy in human experience.

Here, at least, believer and unbeliever can meet on the common ground of being human and of not being satisfied with the human condition as it is experienced. Even those who are most firm in believing that it cannot be altered express discontent at its unalterableness, and this attitude is becoming more widely recognised through the literary expression of the sense of fundamental futility (for example, in Robbe-Grillet and de Clezio, to mention only two). But the Christian expresses this understanding of the human condition to himself in a traditional jargon. The words he uses, like all good jargon, do away with the necessity for explaining and fully analysing on every occasion the concepts which form the given terms of the next stage in the process of discovery. This, the actual living out of the gospel message, is the process that chiefly interests the Christian in a practical way, though it is what he regards as the end of the unfolding of human life that, to him, gives sense and purpose to the whole.

Unfortunately, the words of this useful jargon about the human condition are sometimes used as if they were not just handy symbols for a whole complex and mysterious situation but were actually a sufficient indication of the nature and cause of that situation. (This unjustified promotion of necessary jargon bedevils scientific thought also.) One particular jargon word which is extremely relevant to my purpose is the one that refers to the condition of 'enclosure', of inability to understand oneself or communicate with others, the bitter network of fear and its defences and compensations. All this is covered by the term 'original sin'. Divorced from the state it indicates, given an independent being of its own, it is used not merely to describe but to explain. It acquires implications of guilt, and since the condition of original sin is common to every individual human being from conception, at which point he is obviously not guilty of anything at all, it is thought of as being transmitted in the process of generation, not (as it must be) simply because that is how human beings are, but as if it were an extra 'something'—'stain' is the word most often used—which was handed down from the first pair, who were actually personally 'guilty', to all those who were not but who were thereby condemned to suffer the condition incurred by their progenitors. But as long as the phrase is purely descriptive it does very well. As long as we ask *what* and not *why*, 'original sin' is a good enough answer. It refers to an experienced and verifiable condition in which we feel and know that there is 'something wrong'. If that were all, believer and unbeliever could get on very well. The trouble is that there is a manifest connection, in Christian thought, between this state of 'original sin' and the 'sinful' actions committed by individuals in this state. It is not good enough to say that people in a state of original sin have a natural inclination 'to sin', or to 'misuse' their human nature. Put in that form, it really does not follow so very obviously. To suffer a 'stain', to be 'cut off from the vision of God' (two common ways of expressing the state of fallen man) do not, it would seem, make it unavoidable that individuals should abuse themselves and each other. The whole thing seems quite arbitrary, and this arbitrariness does not worry many convinced Christians because, as I suggested, these inadequate metaphors link up with a reality that they can be said to 'know' in themselves, even to 'experience', (if that word can be divorced from its usual emotional or physical implication) but which seem childish and ridiculous to non-Christians.

So 'sin' turns out to be a barrier to communication, to the search for humanness; it also describes that which fundamentally prevents communication, as I suggested earlier, and is therefore the obstacle to both the idea and the fact of being fully human. Yet on closer examination 'sin' is an idea that does not in itself presuppose any doctrine, even of free will or responsibility. It refers simply to experience. It is this experience which must be defined and so grasped as an idea with real and personal relevance, if we are to get anywhere with an attempt to discover how such a barrier could or should be overcome.

It is the fact and experience of sin that makes it necessary to ask, 'What does it mean to be fully human?' Without this barrier of sin, we would not need to ask, we would know. If human beings were wholly in communication with each other the search for humanness would not be necessary, we would know both our absolute limitations and our ultimate possibilities. As it is, we know neither. This state of 'sin', of not knowing and even being afraid to know, is the *raison d'être* of such a book as this. Therefore it is necessary right at the beginning to examine briefly what we mean by sin as a human fact of experience. The experience of being enclosed I have already discussed. But this condition of enclosure leads, observably, to actions by individuals which harm themselves and others. These actions we call sinful or 'evil', and the idea of evil as a 'thing' has taken possession of the minds and imaginations of men. Yet the Christian position has always been that evil is not a 'thing' at all but an absence, a sort of vacuum of good. Once this is taken seriously, not as a philosophical toy but as a tool for the practical interpretation of human behaviour, the whole idea of sin seems still mysterious, certainly, but not so arbitrary. Evil as the devil, as an actual force in human life, I shall examine in a later chapter. Here, I only want to examine what we mean by sin as lack of communication, as absence.

What follows is an attempt to form a 'picture'—necessarily inadequate—by which it may be possible to think of 'sin' as a reality and yet as an absence. It could be assumed, as a rough hypothesis, that in the process of change from an animal to a human condition the emergent consciousness would tend to be directed to individual phenomena, whether personal or exterior to the person, and that any sort of synthesis of phenomena observed and reflected upon would come later. (This is certainly true of the small child's knowledge.) So that between, as it were, the various intellectual concepts (however simple) that express what is ob-observed, there would be a sort of psychological vacuum. The filling in of some of these 'spaces' in the realm of the understanding of the physical world has been the work of 'science' in the broad sense, and how slow a business it has been, and how many mistakes have been made, is a matter of history. But other kinds of knowledge (that is, ways of bridging over the 'spaces' between the understandings of individual or grouped phenomena) are even less easy to pin down. It is difficult for instance to establish the relation between one's own experienced emotions and those of other people. We can only judge that since the observed behaviour is similar, the underlying emotion must be similar too. In most cases intuitive understandings of another person's emotional state is a more reliable guide than rational deduction from the evidence, and the normal method is a mixture of both.

When the individual, observable components of experience (in the widest sense) are mentally put together in an 'arbitrary' way this is another way of saying that the real organic relationship has not been discovered. What is imposed is a rational, intellectual interpretation, the links which are missing from observation being filled in by symbols which may have a reference to realities beyond the grasp of the conscious imagination but which, in practice, may be endowed with an independent existence, in the form for instance of gods and demons or angels.

This is only one example of the kind of development by which human beings appear to have managed to work out, through the millennia of life on this planet, a way of living with these 'spaces' within the tissue of their mental existence. The spaces have not been eliminated, they appear to have been merely 'grown over'. So these 'spaces', these painful and distorting 'separations' of elements in human life which are of their nature organically connected, have become, it seems, deeply embedded in the very fabric of human nature. The phantoms and bogeys that attempt to bridge the gaps cannot really do so, but have at least helped to make life more rationally comprehensible and therefore more bearable if not more pleasant. But the more successful and complete the process of covering up the 'spaces' has been and the more deeply embedded they have become, the more it becomes essential for the human 'thing' to repel any attempts from outside itself to penetrate this fabric, which may be distorted but yet is closely knit and workable as a means of living an allotted number of years without personal disintegration.

It is 'natural' to man to repel the attacks of another's need— think of the difficulty mentioned above of getting individuals (or nations) to tackle world hunger. There is a space between the *fact* of another man's state of poverty, hunger, grief, and so on, and the emotional equivalent in oneself. This 'space' is filled up by protective imaginary concepts varying according to cultural background, such as 'the will of God', 'charity begins at home', 'misfortune is a punishment for sin', or 'every man for himself'. The currents of human sympathy cannot cross such barriers, which have a definite purpose and in a sense a necessary one. This purpose is to defend the structure of human nature as it exists, for it seems to be the case that to submit to such communication does, in some degree, 'destroy' part of the existing fabric and thereby make access possible to whatever lies on the 'other side' of the previously enclosed 'space'. This seems to be indicated, though by no means convincingly demonstrated, by the fact that once a person has, for instance, laid himself open to another's claims on his compassion he normally continues to be so, unless he becomes aware of some very strong counteracting force in his own life which did not previously affect his behaviour. This new 'counteraction' would be, in effect, the barrier to another 'space' in the fabric and would need a further 'opening up'.

Putting up barriers against others' attacks on one's own life-fabric may help to indicate one kind of 'sinful' behaviour. It gives a clue to such things as selfishness, callousness, pride and all 'excluding' mental habits like snobbery. There are also other, less easily recognisable, forms of self-reassurance like covetousness, vanity, boastfulness and so on. These things help to reinforce the fabric of personality against attacks. 'Greedy' or 'lustful' behaviour also helps to reassure the self of its security (insecure children often eat enormously). The use of sex, however, is ambiguous, for although it is often a 'comfort habit', arising from a need for reassurance of personal existence and power as against another person, it is also linked to the other type of sin which is not protective but aggressive. The need for self-defence does not help to account for definitely aggressive behaviour which looks as if it were not motivated by fear of the destruction of the self but by a desire to destroy another self. Can it all be explained by the residual reactions to the primitive (animal and human) urges used in hunting or self-defence? Perhaps, but this does not explain why certain kinds of aggressive behaviour and not others should be experienced as 'wrong' or disordered, even by the actor, and even though this person may feel that his action was in fact excused by circumstances, made inevitable by his character, or even justified as a means of restoring an unfair balance of power. There is also in many cases a definite element of pleasure in doing something which is recognised as evil, one which is absent in purely self-protective or self-reinforcing sins. A possible explanation could be that the enclosed and more or less accepted 'spaces' in the human fabric nevertheless create a permanent sense of uneasiness, of incompleteness. There is an unquenchable desire to discover the real nature of the organic whole, a 'discovery' which is made impossible by the insulating spaces. But if it is by nature not possible for a person to begin this self-discovery from within himself he has a desire to 'discover' himself through the self of another person and, as I suggested, this is done by tearing apart some of the actual fabric of personality in order to penetrate beyond the enclosing layer of insulating vacuum full of comforting phantasies. The effect of this on the person so attacked may be felt in an equivalent emotion by the attacker, and so create what appears to be a new experience in the attacker's self, one by which he becomes aware of himself in ways which are otherwise closed to him. The inflicting of pain—physical or (much more often) mental—on another human being may be actually an attempt at communication of a very intimate kind. It is often, though not always, associated with sex in the narrow sense of action and feeling directly connected with coitus, and probably always with sex in the wider sense used by some psychologists. The reaction of fear and pain in the other does, sometimes, open up a corresponding layer of emotion in the actor, and in that case the desire to cause pain will be followed by a real 're-union' and a new sense of closeness. Some people only attain a deepened communication by this means, as in the case of married couples who seem to need periodic 'rows' to keep them going. But often enough there is no real openness as a result. The emotion alone is valued and therefore must be constantly repeated in order to regain the sensation. This odd but familiar desire in human life raises one of the biggest questions of all about what human beings are 'really' like. In a recent broadcast a speaker referred to 'man's delight in cruelty for its own sake, the aesthetic satisfaction which he derives from the infliction of pain and the deliberate corruption of the young'.[1] The function of suffering and its relation to communication is discussed in the last chapter of this book. It is mentioned here in the context of 'sin' and its nature as an experience.

Any way of talking about the human condition should make it apparent that the human person is an organic whole, and this I have tried to do by expressing the human condition as one in

[1] Geraint T. Jones, 'Was there a Historic Fall?', *The Listener*, August, 1965.

which the fabric of personality is divided within itself by 'spaces'
that prevent communication and inter-action. But once this image
has been established there are more convenient ways of referring
to this state, and the one used by St Paul is not merely convenient
but completely relevant. The human condition of 'enclosure',
of a personality disintegrated and at odds with itself and with
others, penetrated by the 'spaces' or 'absences' of good which are
what we call evil, but so closely knit around these 'spaces' that to
alter the condition requires a literal destruction: this complex
St Paul refers to as 'the flesh' and the events or actions which
result from this state he calls 'sin'. This way of talking of it
makes it clear that what is wrong with human nature is wrong
with the whole man, not with a separate thing called 'the soul',
whatever that may be. On the other hand it does not mean that the
source of evil is the physical body. The body is, to St Paul, a
thing good in itself but liable to misuse when a man acts 'according
to the flesh'. But it is interesting to notice that St Paul uses, in
one place, a different terminology to express the opposition
between the 'fallen' state of man and the state he 'should' be in.
Instead of using words like 'flesh' and 'spirit' which imply,
though they do not state, that the change from one to the other is
a complete alteration of the 'substance' of personality, he uses a
metaphor that shows clearly an identity of substance between the
two states. He talks of the 'old leaven' of malice and evil, which
must be replaced by a fresh dough, for making an '*un*leavened
bread'. This refers, of course, to the unleavened bread used at
Passover, when 'Christ, our Passover lamb, has been sacrificed'.
But the point, in the context of this study, is that the essential
difference between leavened and unleavened bread lies in the
presence or absence of the little bubbles caused by the working
of the yeast. These bubbles are in the dough itself, so that to get
rid of them would involve actually 'destroying' the dough. But
unleavened bread has no 'bubbles', it is a homogeneous whole
without admixture of any 'foreign substance', hence St Paul
calls it 'unleavened bread of *sincerity* ('without wax' to cover up
faults and flaws) and *truth* (which requires knowledge i.e. com-

munication)'. The connection between this comparison of St Paul's and the 'new' one which I have used is obvious.

If the complex expressed by the Pauline use of 'the flesh' or (in a more limited context) of 'the old leaven' can be taken at this point to indicate sufficiently the human condition as it is experienced, the next question, obviously enough, is 'What, if anything, can be done about it?'.

Some of the conditions of a satisfactory answer are imposed by the understanding of the state to which an 'answer' is required. The conviction that extensions of knowledge of all kinds constitute an 'improvement' in the human lot shows that the answer must lie at least partly in precisely this 'horizontal' or 'quantitative' improvement by all the means available. But the curious and persisting desire for an actual transformation of the mode of human existence shows that a merely 'horizontal' enlargement of the scope of human life is not enough. It is this second kind of 'drive' which presents the greater difficulty in understanding, but the greatest of all is perhaps posed by the need to reconcile the two. The tendency, when faced with these two types of the human endeavour towards 'self-improvement', has been to regard them as mutually incompatible. Transformation as total release has been sought at the expense of ordinary pleasures, ordinary intellectual knowledge, ordinary effort and the achievement of concrete ends. Buddhism is the clearest and most coherent example of a religion based on this view of the proper aim of human life. This attitude is evident also within the stream of orthodox Christian mysticism (the most famous of all 'spiritual' books, *The Imitation of Christ*, is an example) but is more easily recognisable in movements such as the Catharist heresy. Alternatively, limited and 'normal' ends have been sought on the assumption either that complete transcendance of the experienced human condition is impossible and illusory (and the attempt even wicked, treachery to reality) or that it is confined to a favoured minority, whether arbitrarily chosen by fate or transformed by their own mysterious efforts. The former is the assumption on which modern western civilisation is based, the latter accounts for the popularity throughout history of various types of 'holy men' whom no one attempted to imitate.

The idea that the two types of desire for improvement are in fact aiming at the same ultimate goal and so are destined to meet appears to be implicit in the Christian understanding of life. Although it has not been explicitly understood among Christians in general, it has been lived out in practice by many who reject it intellectually, and I have tried to discover the relationship more deeply in chapters five and six of this book.

But if there is any validity in the persisting conviction that human beings really can totally transcend their present manner of existence, and if we can accept the Christian assumption that this transformation must involve the whole man, not merely (as in the gnostic ideal) the 'spiritual' part of him, then it is inescapable that man should not only look forward to but actually work towards a final state in which he will become capable of a new mode of existence, entirely transcending the present one, but following from it as a 'natural' development.

The point at which the horizontal development, pushed as far as it can go in a particular direction, yields 'naturally' to the growth (often violent and sudden) of a 'vertical development' is the moment of the breakthrough of passion, using this word in the sense I have described in chapters four and five. How the momentary glimpses afforded by passion in this sense may link up with the continued labour of creation on the horizontal plane, and finally produce a unity of fully human existence without barriers of any kind, is by definition beyond the reach of the human imagination in its enclosed condition. That it could and will happen is an article of the Christian creed, in fact it could be said that it *is* the Christian creed, since the whole complex of ideas about the meaning of life and the method of living it which Christians express in such words as 'creation', 'redemption', 'grace' is really a proclamation of faith in the end of man and of the revelation in Christ of how to attain it.

But if I am right in assuming that this is what human beings basically desire then the purpose of living could truly be described as an effort to become more fully human, and the end may be called the achievement of a full and complete humanity, a humanity in which each one is able to communicate fully with every other in and through the oneness of life which they share, even now, though at present without more than momentary awareness of it.

The Christian revelation gives precision and purpose and assurance to the inchoate striving of all men for a life that is fully human. On the other hand a rigid interpretation of the great metaphors and symbols that have been used from the beginning to embody and express that revelation has succeeded in making the whole Christian idea seem to the majority of educated people (and through them to millions of less educated ones) at best a comforting illusion to be outgrown and at worst a formidable obstacle to the honest and unselfish thinking that leads to real human progress. And in many cases it is those who reject the Christian idea as they know it who can actually do most to make clear the real human meaning of the faith that Christians profess.

To become holy is to become human. A fully matured and perfected humanity is capable of the vision of God in the life of the resurrection. Here are the traditional Christian terms meeting the humanist ones and both will dislike the encounter and recoil from it. I cannot speak for the humanist, but from the Christian side I say that a Christian who perceives the link between the two cannot recoil from this meeting without betraying his commitment to the Christian vocation. His vocation is to become fully human himself by helping others to achieve a deeper, fuller humanity by all means available. This is what Christians are for, and at this time perhaps we are able to see our vocation as part of the universal striving towards a more complete understanding and living of human life. If the Christian's part in this is a special one, this 'specialness' does not lie in any exclusive claim on the God whom we know only by the love and the need we encounter in others and the craving we know in ourselves. It is 'special' in that each Christian is called to attempt, however feebly, to do the work that Christ did: to serve without tiring, to give without limit,

and to witness by word and act to the hope that makes sense of
the apparently ridiculous aspirations of a race of fear-ridden,
security-craving, suspicious, ambitious and doggedly alive
animals.

CHAPTER I

'SEEK AND YOU SHALL FIND'

The need to search

No discovery is made unless there is at least a minimal will to recognise some new thing, idea, experience, by relating it to those already known. The thing itself may be there, but it remains without meaning or relevance, it is not 'discovered' to the mind, even though some new complex of ideas to which it was the essential clue was being sought. It is only later, perhaps much later, that its relevance becomes dazzlingly apparent. On the other hand the discovery would never have been made at all, the relevance of the apparently irrelevant fact would never have become apparent if the new synthesis, the new intellectual complex, were not being sought. The dramatic discovery of penicillin is a case in point. Some problem requires a solution: it may be a new problem, or it may be one whose old solutions have been undermined by the discovery of new facts. Although the solution cannot be found along any of the recognised lines of research, it still seems to the seeker that there must be a solution somewhere, if only he could find it. There will always be sane and sensible people to assert, with much reason on their side, that the search is a waste of precious energy and enthusiasm, that the sensible and indeed the only right thing to do is to make the fullest use of available and recognised ideas and facts, that there probably is no 'solution' and that anyway it isn't important. The dreamer, the seer, the inventor have always been the butt of jokes, have always been regarded by many practical people as cranky, socially unproductive or mentally deranged. The search for something that cannot be described, since it doesn't yet 'exist' is bound to seem futile to most people, and it can often seem futile to the seeker, too. In moments of discouragement he finds it all too easy to conclude that the others are right, there really is nothing to find, he is pursuing a mirage. Then he sees his sense of purpose as merely obstinacy, his dissatisfaction with the status quo as a foolish vanity, his vigorous desire to be honest and not indulge in facile solutions that fit his own wishes as a delusion of pride worse than the acceptance of a comforting illusion. The agony of the pioneer in any field is described in Kipling's poem 'The Explorer' (the poem's literary merits are beside the point):

'"There's no sense in going further, it's the edge of cultivation."'
So they said and I believed it . . .'

But all the same:

'A voice as bad as conscience rang interminable changes
On one everlasting whisper, day and night repeated—so:
"Something hidden. Go and find it. Go and look behind
the Ranges—
    Something lost behind the Ranges. Lost and waiting
for you—Go!"'

Sometimes the explorer abandons the search and persuades himself that in doing so he is being sensible, humble and far more obviously useful to other people.

The surprising thing is not that some abandon the search but that some go on searching, in spite of inward and outward discouragement, facing a darkness that seems impenetrable with the frail but inextinguishable certainty that there is something to be found, even if they themselves are fated never to find it. And it is on such people that human progress or even continued existence depends, for the refusal to explore and extend the area of understanding leads not, as the fearful and cautious suppose, to the preservation and safety of the existing state but to its eventual destruction by the force of internal energies denied their proper outlet. The great discoveries of the past, whether in natural science, art or philosophy, have all come about because someone was prepared to risk feeling obstinate, proud and deluded, to risk the suspicion of other people, and—worst of all—to risk being ultimately futile, in the pursuit of a truth whose existence could only be, at that stage, a matter of faith. In retrospect they were justified. Galileo, Jenner, Pasteur, the Curies are heroes now. To later generations the object of their blind and painful faith seems clear to the point of obviousness.

The need for unceasing pursuit of scientific or philosophical truth is accepted by most people. The idea that human life as a whole should be—and is—the subject of the same ceaseless search is less easy to accept.

The search for the fullness of being human both for the individual and the race is much more problematic and apparently futile than the search for the next synthesis of hitherto separated lines of thought in any particular field of knowledge. This is so because in the pursuit of scientific knowledge (in the widest possible sense) the intellect only is concerned, though there may be influences and repercussions of an emotional nature. But the search for a fuller kind of understanding of human living is essentially a search for something involving all aspects of being human—physical, emotional, intellectual, moral. Here discoveries can never achieve even the degree of certainty which is accorded to more limited discoveries. The test of the validity of new understandings in the search for human perfection is whether they 'work' as a means of making people, individually and collectively, more able to 'grow up'—that is, better related to each other, more at peace with themselves, more able to adjust to events, in fact 'happier' in a wider sense than that of immediate satisfaction. This is of course the test also of new understandings in any field, for 'certainty' is relative. A new synthesis of ideas makes possible predictions about how events, facts, will behave, develop, relate. It is 'certain' in so far as the predictions based on it turn out to be accurate, in so far as it 'works'. But, by 'working' it, new facts may be uncovered that demand still another search for a further synthesis, a little more 'real' than the last one but never in itself the final one.

An accepted system of thought or morality ceases to 'work' when facts or ideas are found which cannot be made to fit into it. The theories—scientific or theological—that had been used to fill the gaps in direct experience are challenged by new experiences, or explanations of experience, that don't fit the 'shape' of the gaps as explained by the old system, and give rise to new notions of the relationship between experiences, both isolated ones and the complexes, or 'blocks', in which experiences are normally thought of. The first reaction is usually to try to force the new ideas to fit the old patterns, or else to reject them as meaningless or 'wicked' at those points where they cannot be made to fit. This was the initial reaction of Christian orthodoxy to ideas about evolution and to the pioneers of depth psychology.

The reaction of the honest mind, when the new ideas refuse to be fitted in or to disappear, is to try to see exactly what effect they must have in modifying hitherto comfortably workable systems of thought. Inevitably, when the new ideas are really significant and far-reaching, what happens is that the old system comes apart, the hypotheses that had linked the parts no longer seem tenable, there remain only the isolated bits of experience, and in the general upheaval the idea of 'experience' is also liable to be questioned, and for safety's sake may be narrowed down to only those things which are directly perceptible by the senses or can be directly deduced from these by the use of reason. In fact the temptation, in such a situation (and in honesty the situation itself cannot be avoided) is to assume that because the old ideas about the nature of the links between experiences have become untenable, there are therefore no links at all. There are, in that case, only the immediate and obvious needs of daily living to consider, ways of living that produce a reasonable minimum of happiness or at least comfort in an essentially hopeless situation. (Hopeless, not because things are bound to get worse but because there is no clear reason why they should get better.) This hopelessness, this rejection of the search for truth in the name of truth itself, is a new phenomenon. The unbelievers of past generations did not feel like this. Victorian agnosticism had the same moral force and crusading fervour as contemporary non-conformist Christianity. Both waved the banner of truth with complete conviction.

That it is impossible to arrive at truth may seem the obviously sane and honest conclusion, and a fairly satisfactory one, since in spite of its bitterness it leaves room for the enjoyment of most of the good things that human beings have devised for themselves. Also, it provides the support of feeling that one is denying oneself, with the courage of honesty, the comfort other people gain from their illusions.

But the kind of courage required for such an abandonment of hope has as its motto 'divide and conquer'. It attacks by taking things—experiences, and the qualities of people—in isolation, and keeping them in isolation, in which state they are indeed easy to deal with. 'Things as they are' are allowed to combine for immediate practical purposes, because otherwise life is impossible, but the possible implications of their combination, when these implications are not immediately verifiable, are ruled out as meaningless or at least too uncertain to be worth investigation. This was the understandable reaction of many sensitive people after the war. The implications for human nature of war experiences were too frightful to be allowed. It was better to refuse to recognise the human validity of anything but conscious decision. (The fuller exposition of this existentialist reaction belongs to a later chapter). Such an attitude is perhaps more honest than the state of mind which accepts any hypothetical synthesis of experiences that can conceivably make life more meaningful or provide a sufficient motive for the endurance of sorrow and apparent futility. Comparison with this kind of patent self-delusion is what reinforces the 'nothing but' attitude of mind by contrasting such obvious intellectual and moral self-indulgence with its own rather bleak (and therefore, says the puritan in us, more virtuous) philosophy. But in fact there are no grounds for supposing that an idea is right simply because it is dreary, and 'nothing buttery' is basically just as much a rationalisation of emotion as the grasping of emotionally satisfying artificial syntheses, whether 'religious' or not. It is honest and reasonable to say, 'I cannot see any way of linking experiences, beyond the immediate needs of living, which makes sense to me.' But this is not the same as saying: 'There can be no possible sense beyond immediate experience.' Such a statement is essentially as dogmatic as any orthodox Christian one because it excludes from consideration all experiences or hypotheses that appear to conflict with it.

That it is unreasonable to exclude the possibility of a reality beyond the reach of immediate verification is suggested by the typical pattern of discovery itself. The obvious development in all fields is towards a closing of gaps in knowledge. This tendency is clearly aimed at eventually eliminating all the gaps and this possibility is accepted in the area covered by scientific research of all kinds. But if it can be accepted quite happily in this area it seems reasonable to suppose that the gap which is the most enormous of all, that between man's knowledge of his environment (including his physical being) and his knowledge of his own self, could eventually also be closed. In the past, attempts to do this have consisted mainly of hypotheses that questioned the reality of either the one or the other. If the material world is illusion, and destined to disappear when full enlightenment is attained, then there is no problem, no gap, left. If the psyche is ultimately fully explainable in terms of measurable physical cause and effect then there is no problem, no gap, either. Both hypotheses work by rejecting all evidence that does not fit, not because it is clearly invalid or questionable in itself, but just because it does not fit. But if such satisfyingly sweeping solutions are to be rejected (not, be it noted, because they are 'impossible', but because, so far, they do not fit the evidence as it can most easily be understood) it has to be admitted both that at present we cannot possibly see how the gap can be closed and that there is no *a priori* reason for supposing that it cannot be.

But it is immediately clear that it is not enough to say 'perhaps a synthesis will ultimately emerge' and leave it at that. As Simone Weil stressed, the search must be in some sense a passive one, an attitude of attention and waiting rather than action; but mental and spiritual 'activity' are an essential part of this 'attention'. The recognition that there exists the possibility of a final synthesis of human understanding demands a decision. To remain indifferent is not to avoid decision, it is to decide to abdicate responsibility for the achievement of a solution, supposing one to be possible. But the decision to accept the implication of such a possibility is a decision to accept a degree of personal responsibility for pursuing it.

Comparatively few people are explicitly committed to a conscious search for the ultimate meaning of being human. Those who are so committed are distinguished by the fact that not only do they try to live their lives better and learn from experience but they also try to express to themselves what they, and others, experience in living. They compare these experiences and try to discover their interrelation—and how the knowledge of this interrelation can be applied to living in order to make it better, both for themselves and for others. These are 'explicit seekers' and they are able to assist what could be called the 'implicit seekers' to recognise the processes of development in themselves and so progress by the light of this recognition to face the next stage of discovery. The implicit seeker is not primarily concerned with testing the validity of the inherited pattern of living. He lives in it and, without reflecting on it, relates his experiences to it quite happily. It 'works' for him and that is enough. The fact that he is, implicitly, a 'seeker' only becomes apparent when something happens that does not fit his pattern. If he is a 'seeker' he will be willing to test the validity of modified or even quite new experiences or ideas that are offered him by 'feeling' them, to see if they really 'work' in his experience. For him, as for the 'explicit' seeker, there will be a period of darkness when only 'faith' can enable him to hope for some way out. George Eliot describes such an experience in *Felix Holt*, where she traces Esther's struggle against the new experience offered by Felix. She clings to her comfortable pattern, but, being basically honest, is driven in the end to test the experience for herself and see if it 'works' for her. She suffers a period of doubt and uncertainty, but refuses to take an easy way out, one which fits her former pattern. But if the seeker finally refuses to search he will either distort experience to make it fit his familiar pattern (as Esther found that she would have to do if she married Harold Transome) or he will assume that thereafter no pattern is valid at all. To do either of these things is to abandon the search. To do either of them may seem to be the realistic course in face of the apparently impenetrable ignorance that surrounds human living, and the fact that it is wrong to do either of these things can only become apparent by observing the results: loss of the sense of human value, a growing feeling of futility contained only by rigid beliefs (which become increasingly unrelated to living) or by the necessities of daily existence and the momentum of habit and social custom. Neither of these is, in the end, sufficient to maintain real human living. The observable results of this in our own civilisation is a frantic search for an easy way out of a situation that has become unbearable, an escape rather than a way through. Sex and drugs, the pursuit of money and power and pleasure, become means of suppressing the gnawing sense of futility instead of means of perhaps breaking through (at whatever risk) to a newer kind of reality. In some cases suicide can be the final acknowledgement that neither dogma nor routine nor temporary unconsciousness has been enough to prevent the discovery of all absence of meaning in human life. The more common solution is retreat into cynicism and apathy, like a snail into its shell.

The continual search, explicit or implicit, is the condition of continued growth. The condition of continued search is an act of faith, an assertion in the face of all experience and common sense that there is something to be found which has not yet been found. This is something that Christ knew and said, it is of the essence of his message, for without it humanity must die. An act of faith is required of both believer and unbeliever if they are to be seekers at all. It makes no difference whether the forms in which they express to themselves the obligation to search contain a theistic premise or not. The dividing line here is not between one who accepts certain propositions about the nature of reality beyond the reach of immediate experience (though by definition not of any possible experience) and one who does not. Rather, on one side of the line are those who are prepared to commit themselves to attempt to *discover* the nature of that reality as far as they are able, thus testifying to a faith, however intellectually incredible, that such a reality at least could exist. On the other side are those who either refuse to admit the possibility of any reality but immediate experience (though accepting certain convenient patterns of thought and behaviour as necessary for continued living), or who use such a pattern, accepted in an arbitrary fashion even though it may be explained as reasonable. They use it not as a basis of living from which new adventures may be made but as a substitute for any adventure at all. In this sense, then, the 'believer' is one who is prepared to risk this act of faith, and he can be a Christian or he can be an atheist. Likewise the 'unbeliever' in this sense is the one who refuses the act of faith and he also can be an atheist, but he can also be a Christian in the sense of one who professes belief in certain propositions about the revelation of God in Christ. On the face of it, it might seem that a 'believer', in this sense of one who will commit himself to search, would be more likely to be a Christian than an atheist. This might be so on the basis of the psychological compatability of Christian beliefs and faith in the possible fullness of being human, for this is what Christ frequently referred to as the 'Kingdom of Heaven'. But in practice the historical forms of Christianity (which can be historically justified as stages of development) have provided a considerable barrier to any such belief. It would be hard to say, just from observation, whether more Christians or more agnostics or atheists are 'believers' in this sense.

The need to search is fundamental to the teaching of Christ, but if Christ's ideas on the subject of human development are to be shown to be a possible guide to the search of 'believers' in my sense—whatever their theological standpoint—then this contribution must be one which clearly provides something indispensable at every stage of the discovery, both intellectually and spiritually. This he claimed to do.

At first sight it would seem impossible for anyone who had not first made an act of faith in the supreme authority of Christ to take him as a guide worthy of trust. But in fact his contemporaries

did not become his followers by making such an act of faith. To
those who met him he was a man, no more, and it was only by
observing his behaviour and listening to him that men came to
the point where they were willing to believe in him. Their belief,
even then, was a very limited and cloudy one, consciously related
to nationalistic hopes for a Jewish kingdom and various immediate
benefits from it. But this was enough. He did not ask for special
consideration, he asked to be judged on his merits. 'Seek and you
shall find,' he told his disciples, and he did not tell them what they
would find. He only told them that *he* knew, and that they could
take it from him that there was something to find. In fact he said
quite explicitly that it was quite useless to expect clear directions
or tests in the discovery of his Kingdom. His coming, he said,
would be like a lightning flash, lighting up the whole sky quite
suddenly, and this is in fact what the stages of any discovery are
like, as a matter of experience. The sudden flash of enlightenment
is familiar to most people, in little matters as in great ones.

Although this light is not simply an interior enlightenment, it is
first of all interior. 'The eye is the lamp of the body. So, if your
eye is sound your whole body will be full of light.' If you see
(look outwards) clearly, judge honestly by the 'light' which
comes from the courageous commitment to search, you will get
to know yourself truly. (Esther in *Felix Holt* is again an excellent
example.) 'If your eye is not sound, your whole body will be
full of darkness.' When a man refuses to see honestly (with the
'eye' that looks outwards) he is shut in with his own fantasies and
his judgement of everything, inside and outside, will be distorted
and in 'darkness'. So Othello became incapable of 'seeing'
Desdemona, but substituted a phantom of his own mind. But
light is for communication: 'Let your light so shine before men
that they may see your good works and glorify your Father who is
in heaven.' In terms of ordinary living this means that if you are
really looking for truth your own discoveries about it will affect
your behaviour, will make you 'clearer' to other people so that
they will see the point of being committed to something more
than getting through life from day to day without actual harm or

misery, and will be encouraged in their own efforts. Light, in fact, is essentially a communal thing; it is of its nature to be shared.

St John's gospel is fond of the 'light' metaphor. The famous introduction has light as its main theme. The 'life' which Christ came to bring (equivalent to what the synoptic gospels call 'the Kingdom of Heaven') is itself described as 'light' and this is linked to the idea of Christ as the 'Word'. Both 'word' and 'light' imply knowledge, and show that this 'life', the life of the Kingdom of Heaven, is not delivered complete but is to be known, discovered, made clear, by means of the 'light' which Christ brought. But this light only enlightens those who can accept it, and many do not. 'The world knew him not', in particular 'his own people received him not', a state of affairs which unfortunately continues among those called by his name now. But to those who did 'receive him', who committed themselves to the unknown Kingdom, 'he gave the power to become the children of God' which is equivalent to 'entering the Kingdom' in the other gospels. And these men who are 'sons of God' are in their turn lamps for others, like John the Baptist whom Christ called 'a burning and shining lamp'. But even those who 'rejoice for a while in the light' may turn against it and those who carry it and live by it must be prepared for the enmity of those who are wilfully blind, like the Pharisees who threw out the blind man who was healed. Christ condemned them, not for being blind, which perhaps they could not help, but for saying 'we see', and so misleading others. 'Blind guides' he called them, 'and when the (culpably) blind lead the (inculpably) blind they both fall into the ditch'. It may be unfair, but that is how it is, as Hitler's Germany demonstrated for us.

The man who called himself 'the light of the world' used this phrase to claim unique knowledge about the proper development of human life, its purpose and end. This claim is made in various forms throughout the gospels and reiterated in all the apostolic letters and records. It is one for which neither Christ nor his followers offered any proof except the authentication given it by the hearts of men who heard his words and observed his actions.

At this crisis of history there is an odd similarity between the state of the unbeliever, cut off from the Gospel by the need to reject (whether rightly or wrongly) known forms of institutional Christianity, and the believer who is still bound by love to one of these forms and is thereby also deprived of an unprejudiced view of the gospel of Christ. In these situations the advantage, if there is one, probably lies on the side of the unbeliever. He is to some extent free to form his own opinion of Christ's message without being forced constantly to consider whether this or that understanding of what Christ said is or is not compatible with the accepted formulations of the Christian Church, and if it is not, whether the personally achieved understanding is wrong or whether the Church's traditional interpretation has been wrong. (Perhaps this analysis of the situation, from one who is a believer, underestimates the difficulties of the unbeliever, who also suffers from a dead weight of inherited personal prejudices, though of a different kind.)

The unbeliever with rooted (and probably justified) anti-Christian prejudices, and the believer conscious of the worth of an established traditional form of religion but intellectually and morally nauseated by the distortions of truth that have become embedded in it during the course of history both have their difficulties in judging honestly the extraordinary claims of Christ, but their difficulties are no greater than those that faced his contemporaries. And it is essential to realise that he did not then and could not now demand of anyone an 'act of faith', in the sense of an abandonment of the use of reason, or normal judgment, or moral discrimination or any of the ordinary means by which we form an opinion or reach a decision. All that he ever asked of a man was that he should be honest with himself, willing to see and hear with his heart as well as his eyes and ears. He must desire the truth; that is all.

If all that is required for a man to enter the Kingdom of Heaven be an open heart and a mind as far as possible detached from prejudice, how is it that the centuries during which very many men have come to Christ in this frame of mind have produced in the name of Christ such a revolting hotch-potch of magic, superstition, tyranny, hatred, fear, legalism and stupidity? The fact that all this nastiness has not prevented the appearance of an unending procession of men and women of unmistakable human magnificence does not remove the nastiness, it merely makes the loveliness surprising. Did these people—the canonised saints and the thousands of un-canonised ones—develop as they did in spite of the forms of Christianity they accepted or because of them? The question must be put thus because it is clear that they nearly always did accept Christianity in exactly the same forms, with the same distortions, as their contemporaries. Their prejudices were the same, they were often deeply attached to the same magical practices and wildly superstitious beliefs as the people among whom they lived. It is true that their living of Christianity often compelled them to revolt against some aspect or other of contemporary life which seemed incompatible with the Gospel, but this revolt nevertheless followed a pattern explicable in terms of the currently accepted beliefs and traditions of Christian behaviour. This applies as much to those who broke away from the Catholic tradition as to those who worked for reform within it. When the area in which reform was demanded was one that contradicted some belief or custom that appeared to be essential to the Catholic tradition of Christianity, then the reformer's impetus took him out of the Church. In other areas of theology and practice the original reformers, whatever further divergences may have appeared among their successors, accepted quite happily many of the opinions and customs of the Church they had left. But this does not apply to the many smaller sects which have sprung up from time to time and which threw out, between them, nearly every recognised Christian doctrine in favour of millennial aspirations and esoteric symbolic ritual with a dash of witchcraft. These curious movements may well represent a valid revolt against the overconscious clarity of institutional religion, but as a matter of history they do not appear to have produced many people of outstanding human excellence, and they seem to have ended generally in bloodshed and madness, as in the case of the various millennial heresies of the Middle Ages.

Both these facts are interesting: the fact that outstanding Christians (canonised or not) usually concentrated their desire for reform in one area, either theological or more often moral, and accepted the rest of current Christianity, and the fact that attempts to get right below the surface and find a 'short cut' to salvation did not produce very good results by normal human standards.

It looks as if there must be something in the gospel message which 'works' even when the reasons for its working are understood in pseudo-magical terms, and which do not work when the clear-cut, literal message is ignored in favour of symbolic interpretations that aim at getting 'below the surface' without benefit of 'above the surface' intelligence and moral behaviour. The system 'works' as a child blindly obeying his mother's directions in elementary cookery finds that the recipe 'works', though he has no idea how and may invent fanciful reasons of his own.

But further progress can continue only so far by the use of a system that is made to work without clear understanding. After a certain point it must be better understood or progress is blocked. The attempts to understand may appear to be destructive and are therefore feared. In certain ages the general intellectual understanding of Christianity was temporarily so well in accord with the general state of knowledge that there was little or no conflict between them. In such ages (the early Middle Ages for instance) the search for a deeper understanding was most likely to be carried forward into areas of moral darkness. The Franciscan reform was of this kind, a push against the growing worldliness of existing institutional religion. The Wesleyan movement also was not so much a revolt against false theology—the theological division was widened later—as an attempt to throw the light of Christ into the dreary dusk created by too tidy, too rational, and too complacent a version of Christianity. In both cases—and many others—the revolt was against a restriction of the need to discover the Kingdom of Heaven, to live in a way that gave room to develop all that goes to make up a human being.

In ages when intellectual speculation, whether theological (as at the Reformation) or scientific (as in the nineteenth century), was developing ideas that did not accord with the currently accepted orthodoxy, two quite different reactions are apparent among those who search. One is a desire to re-interpret the accepted teaching intellectually, trying to discover the relationship between it and the new ideas. This, historically, was easier for non-Catholic Christians. For Catholics it often led to actual excommunication (as in the Modernist crisis) or to isolation and suspicion (as in the case of Newman). But the ideas bred by people like Tyrrell and Newman have been re-adopted and developed by others in the tradition that rejected them, the teaching of Luther is being discovered by Catholics and that of Catholic theologians by people of the Protestant tradition. And those whose assessment of the meaning of the knowledge brought by scientific discovery obliged them to abandon Christian belief altogether are finding that real Christian ideas throw light on much of human life, while Christians are finding that the search-lights provided by 'secular' science vastly illuminate their understanding of Christianity. But there are many who are searching for what Christ called the Kingdom of Heaven but are not equipped by education or tradition to carry the light of intellectual adventure. They have been known to react to new ideas by turning away into apparent obscurantism, 'ignorant piety' and 'superstitious practices'. And in their murky little corners, wielding inefficient lanterns of uncouth manufacture, they have succeeded in throwing a light of sheer, splendid goodness that has put to shame the acetylene lamps of the inspired but rather terrifying demolition squads of science. Of such a kind were the Curé d'Ars, Thérèse of Lisieux, Damien of Molokai. Charles de Foucauld, patiently saying Mass in the Sahara among unresponsive Tuaregs, made no attempt at actual achievement, but blazed a trail for many. The search for the truth that makes a way of life 'work' is not a monopoly of the intellect.

In their more exalted rank these two kinds of searchers for the Kingdom of Heaven, these apparently incompatible torch-bearers in their pursuit of perfect humanness, correspond to the more ordinary kinds of people who, distrustful of each other as they may be, are looking for something they cannot see. In both cases

some will pursue the search mainly by practical action, and some
by withdrawal and reflection. These have parallel dangers. Where
the former is too complete the danger is from overly 'conscious'
living, legalism, superficiality and smugness; where the latter is
over indulged you get what is sometimes known as 'fancy religions',
witchcraft, drug and sex-cults, or an attitude of indifference to
suffering. These two extremes are the temptations of Western
and Eastern religion respectively.

These divergent attitudes can cease to be incompatible, can
redress any unbalance and remain effectively human in their
search. And they not only can but do achieve this when the teaching
of Christ is taken as a guide.

There have been people of both kinds throughout Christian
history. They quoted him, they prayed to him, they made their
appeal to him as their justification. They tried to live by his
standards, even when these were known through a veil of obscuring
tradition. And even through this veil they succeeded, over and over
again. When they failed it was because they had lost sight of him,
or kept only some limited aspect of his teaching that suited their
purpose when taken out of context, for the Christian way only
'works' as a whole, even when the whole is not understood.
Selected extracts may make an elegant anthology; as a guide to
living they are useless.

Even those who rejected Christ in the pursuit of truth were
obeying him, since what they rejected was a distortion they could
not in conscience accept. The light they carried was the light of
desire for truth, which was his idea of what light is for. They kept
their faith in the search for truth, and found no inconsistency or
dishonesty in doing so.

In the long and often shameful history of the Christian West,
every case where men and women have done something really
and obviously and humanly good can be shown to be in accordance
with the real teaching of Christ, even if at the time it appeared to
be an abandonment of Christianity as generally understood. And
in every case those who so acted were people who had drawn
their goodness from a Christian tradition which carried his message

encased in crude and fantastic forms of thought, decked with relics and arithmetical notions of salvation perhaps, but, in spite of them, clear, unmistakable, speaking straight to the heart that can listen.

If this is so it is perhaps not unreasonable for those who recognise the need for a search for humanness to examine Christ's ideas about it, however little they may be able to accept some of the claims made on his behalf by the historical Church. And it would be well for Christians to look again at the gospel message and discover what it really has to say about the meaning of being human.

CHAPTER II

'OF SUCH IS THE KINGDOM OF HEAVEN'

The conditions for the beginning of freedom

IN the last chapter I examined the drive to discovery which is the
condition of human growth. But the achievement of that maturity
or 'wholeness' for which man is searching depends to a great
extent on the ideas and attitudes acquired in childhood. It is for
this reason that the first questions that must be asked of the Christian message are concerned with childhood, its needs and nature,
with education, and with the relevance of childhood and education
to grown-up attitudes.

'The Kingdom of Heaven' is a phrase which the gospels use in
all sorts of contexts, as a shorthand description of the kind of
human perfection towards which Christ wanted to guide his
followers. It is a very rich and flexible concept which is always
being developed in new ways and examined from different angles.
But perhaps the most famous use of the phrase is one in which
Christ imposes a baffling condition on the attempt to be fully
human. 'Whosoever does not receive the Kingdom of Heaven as a
little child shall not enter it.'

Since human development obviously begins with childhood this
saying is worth examining in two directions; to see what it reveals
about childhood and the needs of the child if he is to grow up to
be as fully human as his capacities allow, and also to see what
childhood has to say about the lifelong attitudes demanded of
anyone who, explicitly or implicitly, is seeking the fullness of
being human, the 'Kingdom of Heaven'. I have here put together
the phrases 'the fullness of being human', and 'the Kingdom of
Heaven' without giving any reason for equating them. The validity
or invalidity of the equation is precisely what needs to be discovered
and the confrontation of the two ideas at every stage will make

it apparent whether or not there is a real correspondence or even identity between them.

The most common interpretation of this saying is that the Kingdom of Heaven can only come to those who are prepared to accept it blindly and passively, relying on the authority of Christ who speaks for his Father. A child accepts what his elders tell him as 'gospel' (this use of the word shows in itself how popular usage treats Christ's words as something people are expected to accept without question) and the quoted phrase is taken to mean that this is the proper attitude for a believer. You have to believe in Christ as a child believes in his parents before you can be a candidate for the Kingdom of Heaven. The unquestioning trust of a child is the condition for entering the Kingdom preached by Christ.

If this is a correct interpretation it immediately excludes from the Kingdom of Heaven all those who have any doubts about the Christian revelation, or even experience difficulties in the full acceptance of it. It does not, of course, imply that they may not 'overcome' doubts or difficulties and fully accept the proffered revelation, but it does seem to mean that the 'receiving' of the Kingdom must be nothing but an act of blind trust. In that case Christ would seem to have considered that, ideally, a child should accept without question all that his parents tell him.

But it seems to me that this interpretation is mistaken. It is possible to reject Christ's teaching and even to question his historical existence but it is not possible to read the gospels and suppose that the man whose message is proclaimed in them was stupid or insensitive or had a mind divorced from the realities of life. If he used a child's attitude to life as the model for those who aspired to 'enter the Kingdom of Heaven' he based it on an accurate and sympathetic observation of real children. The fact that he liked children and they him and that he noticed how they behaved is clear enough from other details recorded in the gospels. If we want to get a real idea of what he considered the value of being 'childlike', then we must, as he did, observe real children. And this will throw light not only on the attitudes proper to an adult who wants to 'enter the Kingdom' (develop fully as a human being) but also perhaps on the way in which the qualities of actual children should be understood and assisted in their development.

Children do, observably, 'believe in' their parents, and therefore 'believe' what they say. This state of belief, leading to acceptance of individual 'beliefs', constitutes the relationship, when it is a good one, of child to parents. It is, in fact, a relationship of belief. The physical oneness of mother and unborn child is first modified to become the combined physical/emotional bond of breast feeding or its equivalent. It develops into a link which is intellectual and emotional and gradually less physical, though the need for reassurance of the reality of the link by re-establishing physical contact from time to time remains, and its final abandonment is retarded if for any reason the emotional bond is threatened. The intellectual aspect of the link becomes increasingly important because the mother, and then both parents, are the child's gateway to the outer world. He feels able to come to grips with it because it is mediated to him through the minds of those who are only gradually becoming distinct from himself. His state of belief is absolute, unless something happens to shatter it. The parents do not help him to understand, rather they *are* his understanding of matters which extend beyond, though they begin in, his immediate experience. They are also the test of the validity of each new experience; they not only explain, extend and link it with other experiences (sometimes by means of ideas that are still meaningless to him), they give him some sort of assurance that the experience is real and that it belongs to one category of experience or another —it 'hurts' or it is 'fun' or it is 'a pity'.

But this basic acceptance, in which the parents seem to be extensions of the child's self and there is no sense of division, is only one part of the child's state in relation to his parents. The other, which becomes increasingly important, is the attempt to disentangle himself from his parents and discover himself in relation to his environment. He does this not by refusing 'belief'— the state of drawing life and understanding from the parents without any sense of separateness—but by feeling for a knowledge of the things he experiences which is his own, a possession that defines him as a person separate from his parents. He asks 'Why?' constantly, and more often than not the 'Why?' is meaningless as an actual question, it is an expression of the fact that the child now knows that his experience is incomplete—not objectively as an event, but subjectively, in that he has not been able to assimilate its significance or make it completely part of himself.

The reiterated 'Why?' is both a symptom of this sense of incompleteness, of uneasiness in relation to exterior reality, and an affirmation of a determination to do something about it. At the same time it is an act of faith in the fact that something can be done about it. The child's 'faith' depends on continuing 'belief' in the parents as sources of life and knowledge. It is generally on them, though by extension on other trusted grown-ups, that the 'whys' of childhood are inflicted, and it is only the basic 'belief' in them that makes it possible to ask 'Why?' about experiences which they have verified, that is, made available to him as real, as objects for his consideration, outside himself. His 'selfness' by which he can ask 'Why?' is derived from them and he expects them to support it during the stage of its incompleteness. If they refuse this support by consistently blocking his attempts at discovery with refusals or mockery or irritation he will gradually cease to ask, and much patient work will be required later on from anyone who wants to re-establish the lost confidence in 'self-hood' by giving a quasi-parental support to new attempts at self-discovery by way of the exploration of the exterior world.

So the 'childlike' attitude that Christ demanded of would-be inheritors of the Kingdom is not merely one of acceptance. Certainly the initial 'act of faith' establishes a oneness that is essentially 'unquestioning'. It is the state of belief, the medium in which questions can be asked. It is not an intellectual abdication but an act of love. It should set free the intellect to explore with confidence new regions, both interior and exterior, just as a child's confidence in his parent's love sets him free to question. The child who is unsure of his parents, a child whose 'belief' has been shaken, is much less able to make new ventures. He tends to learn only with reluctance and difficulty, both intellectually and emotionally.

The initial acceptance, then, is only the first step. It is the condition of the development of a complete relationship, and this relationship must develop by asking questions, by exploring new things and ideas and the relation between them. This 'questioning' is of course not merely intellectual but involves the whole person, and indeed is really part of the process of discovering who and what the person is in himself. Therefore when Christ said that in order to enter the Kingdom it was necessary to change and become like a child he was not saying that his disciples must simply swallow whole whatever he chose to offer them, but rather that they must have in him the kind of confidence and 'oneness' that abolishes distinction between subject and object of 'belief', and that this would enable them to begin a real discovery of themselves as human beings.

He was also saying, by implication, that this kind of attitude in a child is a good thing, something to be preserved and fostered. On another occasion he even said that anyone who 'scandalised' one of these little ones would be better dead. Clearly it seemed vital to him that a child should not lose the state of belief or trust that makes his self-discovery possible. The whole tenor of his remarks about children, in particular his rebuke to the disciples who tried to keep them away from him, shows that 'scandalising' meant frightening them, making them 'close up' and lose the ability to trust which is the condition of proper development.

Two of the parables that illustrate Christ's ideas about the Kingdom show even more clearly the importance of asking 'Why?', of developing and using the basic relationship of trust. They also show that there is no question of simply holding on to something already known. In the parallel though interestingly different stories of the pounds and the talents the King (or Master), about to go away, entrusts money to his servants during his absence. In one story the sums are equal, in the other, unequal, but in both cases the servants who risked losing the money in order to increase it were praised, whereas the one who was afraid of losing the money and therefore simply wrapped it up in a handkerchief, or buried it, was severely blamed. Both versions show that what had been handed over to be used had remained, in this case, not only unused but unexamined. And the result is the same in both cases— the cowardly and resentful servant loses even the original sum, whereas those who had risked their money, and gained more with it, are given not merely a share in what they have gained but something far more than, and different from, the thing originally entrusted to them.

These two parables are usually taken to mean that followers of Christ should not fail to make the fullest use of their abilities and possessions in the service of God. It does not seem to be noticed that Christ often used money, or riches (treasure in a field, or a precious pearl, for instance) as a symbol of the Kingdom of Heaven which human beings desire. What the servants in these stories received was the same thing that must be received 'as a child' by his disciples—that thing which is the condition and true beginning in them of the 'Kingdom of Heaven'. The servant who, in the end, was rejected was one who merely accepted what was given, made only the initial act of faith, and then, because he was afraid, did not 'question' what he had, did not develop it or use it or even look at it.

It seems clear from this that the common Christian tendency to try to protect the faith of a child or young person by insulating him from contacts with ideas that do not seem to support it is not really in keeping with the ideal that Christ put before his disciples. The 'Kingdom of Heaven' which has been 'received' is also to be 'entered', and 'entering' is an action, it implies something willed and quite conscious. The child who is trained to regard his faith as a possession to be guarded will lose it: this is the inescapable lesson. He may, of course, retain the 'shell', he may think he has 'kept the faith', but in the end he will discover that there is nothing there, 'even that which he hath shall be taken away'. This is not a threat but simply the statement of a sequence of psychological cause and effect. The using of 'the Kingdom' is the condition of its continued existence, because it is in the nature of the thing entrusted to grow and change.

The fact that it changes beyond all recognition is shown in

some other images of the Kingdom that Christ used, for instance that of the leaven in the lump of dough. The original bit of leaven is not only much smaller than the finally risen batch of dough, it looks quite different. Even clearer is the example of the grain of mustard seed, which is not only tiny but at first sight utterly unrelated to the great bush in which 'all the birds of the air' can comfortably roost.

Christ apparently wanted his followers to realise that the reward of their efforts would be out of all proportion to either the amount of 'material' initially entrusted to them, or to the effort they put into using it. At the same time he thought of the two as being related, as the seed and the tree are related. The command: 'Trade till I come' includes the two essential elements in human development according to the mind of Christ: money to trade with, and the trading; the seed and its nourishment and consequent growth; the leaven and the kneading and resting of the dough.

The second element is the easier to see and accept. The opening out of the mind and heart, the grasping and using of new ideas and relationships, are the proper aims of all education, and it is only the historically conditioned timidity of certain kinds of Christianity that makes Christian educators set bounds to this opening out for fear of endangering 'faith', considered as a possession. But although at the same time the process of learning both intellectually and emotionally depends on the child's state of 'belief' in his parents or their later substitutes, this belief itself will be endangered if it is not developed. Those parents who try to preserve an image of personal impeccability, infallibility and perfect justice long after the child has passed the stage where such qualities seem to him inevitably attributable to those in whom he believes, will certainly forfeit the child's 'belief' altogether. But if the child is encouraged and allowed to rediscover his parents as real people, human beings with limitations and faults, who love him, he will retain his 'belief' in them, he will keep that confidence which is unquestioning because there is no 'space' in which questions are relevant or meaningful. So that while it is perfectly right and 'real' that the very small child should regard his parents as being of limitless power and goodness, since at this stage such a 'feeling' (never a 'thought') about them is simply the natural expression of his sense of oneness with them, it is also necessary and right that he should gradually discover something more of the nature of the real oneness, which does not in fact depend on the applicability to his parents of any easily understood concepts such as absolute 'fairness' or universal knowledge. It would be ridiculous to say that the small child's absolute belief in his parents was wrong and equally ridiculous to say that the later, more mature 'belief', which is not dependent on ignorance of their limitations, is a loss of faith or shows disrespect or disloyalty. The early 'belief' interprets the love of the parents for the child in terms that are easily understood. The later 'belief' knows that it does not know, that the parents are 'other' and as such not to be comprehended in such simple terms. They are not, in fact, to be totally comprehended at all. The more mature 'belief' involves a certain acceptance of ignorance about them, the acknowledgment that there is much that is baffling, perhaps even repulsive, about the appearance they present, but that one can love them, 'believe' in them, just the same or perhaps even more. If this act of acceptance of ignorance is refused then belief comes to an end, because the parents are reduced to totally comprehensible entities, an arrangement of virtues and vices, information and ignorances, neatly laid out and connected. This leaves no room for the act of faith that is an adherence to a wholeness which, however clear-sighted one may be about its parts, is in itself never comprehensible but only apprehensible, and to which therefore one can only be 'oned' by the act of faith. Faith is by definition prepared to accept incomprehension, and might even be described as an act of embracing incomprehension.

When Christ demanded 'childlikeness' of his followers he was not therefore asking them to arrest their spiritual development at a stage comparable to that of the child who still finds it natural to 'feel' his parents as omnipotent and infallible—that is, at a stage when he can (or would, if he could put his feelings into words) express his oneness with them in terms which are intellectually satisfying only because of his very limited experience of his environment. Nor, when he warned against 'scandalising' a child, was Christ suggesting that children should be protected from influences that would challenge the first simplicity of their expression of their belief. He was condemning the brutal and sudden breaking of that simple intellectual acceptance which destroys not merely the inevitably temporary intellectual structure but the trust which it expressed and which needed it. Such a break means that the child becomes isolated, literally 'made an island', and this isolation is caused by a 'stumbling block'(*skandalon*) put between the child and those to whom he was attached by belief, faith, love, or whatever word best expresses the sense of oneness.

These ideas apply to the development of the child's relationship with his parents, but of course they do not end there because the parent-child relationship creates the conditions for the development of other relationships, both with people and with ideas. 'Ideas' in this connection does not mean merely intellectual concepts but also, and more importantly, whole complexes of attitudes and behaviour patterns which are new and different from the original, limited, 'home' one. It is not necessary or indeed usual for the impact of these to be consciously expressed or intellectually recognised, any more than the impression made by a new person in one's life needs to be described in order to be a valid experience. The reaction to the newcomer, be it a person or a way of living or thinking, depends primarily on whether the child has been able to maintain the state of belief or whether he has become isolated. If his belief is strong and real, at whatever stage of development, he can approach new things with confidence, with a view to establishing the same kind of relationship of 'belief' with them. The 'bridge' is already there. If he has become isolated he is likely to be wary and suspicious; after all, he has to cross the dividing sea, and that is difficult and dangerous. But if the new thing or person can show itself sufficiently inviting he may be induced to build a new bridge of belief, though it may not be as strong as he thinks and is often built, at first, on rather flimsy foundations.

Among the 'new' ideas which are presented to a child are those connected with religion and morality. It is probably in the field of religious education, in the broad sense, that there appears to be the deepest division between the attitudes of the Christian and the unbeliever. The Christian takes it for granted that the child must be taught the basic Christian doctrines and moral precepts as soon and as clearly and urgently as his intellectual and emotional development allows. The intelligent Christian will realise that the teaching will have to be understood more subtly and interpreted with more complexity as the child grows, but the 'givenness' of a body of teaching is assumed. The unbeliever, on the other hand, is likely to say that a child should not be taught any religious ideas as 'given'. He should be taught to base his morality on a developing understanding of the needs of others and the consequent need to modify his own desires in their favour, and should be encouraged to acquire the basis for a philosophy of life, however vague, by learning about the human heritage of religious ideas developed in different times and places. Whether this last is done with reverence for the achievement of the human mind and heart (even if the conclusions are objectively denied) or with pity or scorn for past delusions which have been or should be abandoned, is a matter of the individual attitude of the parents. It should be noticed in passing that the former leaves the child in contact with the aspirations of other men, even if he cannot accept the forms in which they are expressed, while the latter cuts him off from them, 'isolates' him. It may be considered that this isolation is necessary and beneficial, or at least the lesser of two evils, but however this may be, this is what, observably, happens in these two cases. Christian parents who inculcate scorn for non-Christian beliefs, or even for the beliefs of other brands of Christianity, are isolating their children in the same way.

Christ showed recognition of a stage when the initial state of belief is expressed in moral and intellectual terms which are easily comprehensible and form an emotionally and intellectually satisfying complex for the time being. This stage demands that morality shall be fixed and obviously 'fair', and does not easily appreciate, for instance, the point of unrequited generosity. Theological ideas will tend to be ones which are easily understood in terms of simple personal experience. God is 'angry' or 'pleased'. The very arbitrariness of God's rules and reactions are satisfying because they fit in with the pattern by which experience is mediated to the child through his parents before he is in a position to make any judgment on them by comparison with things experienced personally. This applies both to the individual child and to communities at an early stage of religious development. Christ's understanding of this stage, and of its temporary character, explains an apparent contradiction in his teaching about the attitude to morality proper to the Kingdom. He denied that he had come to abolish the Law. The Law, or Torah, did not mean to the Jews simply a set of rules; the word refers to the whole interrelated body of teaching about God and man, about how the chosen people should live and how their history showed the developing relationship between Israel and her God. Far from destroying all this Christ proclaimed that anyone who tried to destroy any detail of it would be 'least in the Kingdom of Heaven'. And yet he could also say of John the Baptist—who summed up all that was best in the Law and the prophets, who was 'more than a prophet' and for whom Christ obviously had the deepest respect and affection—that he who was 'least in the Kingdom of Heaven' was greater than he. So, in the mind of Christ, the Law and the religious state it expressed were so indispensable that to undervalue them showed a lack of understanding that made a true grasp of the meaning of 'the Kingdom' very hard. But although the Law was so necessary it was merely a condition of something infinitely better, so that John, its final and finest product, was still only able to grasp uncertainly at the meaning of the Kingdom Christ had come to preach.

We can put beside this Christ's sweeping statement that it really does not matter whether men worship at Jerusalem or 'on this mountain', because true worshippers must worship 'in spirit and in truth', a saying which appeared to brush away the core of Jewish religious life in the Temple that symbolised the whole vocation and heritage of the chosen people. From both these sayings it seems that Christ loved and valued the Law, but as a temporary expression of something much greater, something related to the 'real thing'—the spirit and truth—as the seed is related to the tree. All of which should not lead any sensible person to despise the seed.

Any attempt to apply Christ's ideas to education should be scrupulously careful to respect this first stage of spiritual development, in the child as in the community.

But the child's security in this framework is only a means to an end. Having grown up as far as possible with its support, he needs to break out of it. He can do this with confidence because he has grown up in it at his own pace until he was ready to discover something better. For some time his excursions into new regions of thought and into new relationships will be punctuated by returns to his 'home' environment in order to renew the confidence he draws from his continued oneness with the source of his life. This applies both to his relations with his parents and with his God, and in spite of the fact that in *both* cases his ideas are 'mistaken', or limited because of his undeveloped intellectual and emotional abilities. In these 'returns' he tests his new discoveries by references to his 'home' ideas, and by doing so he modifies both his new impressions and his understanding of his spiritual home. But the balance gradually changes. At first he judges his new discoveries by how well they fit his 'home' ideas, later he begins to judge his 'home' by the new ideas which, as they increase, are beginning to fit together into complexes which make sense quite apart from how they fit into the 'home' system.

This happened in the larger sphere of religious development when the early Church, beginning to reach out to new ideas, discovered other philosophical systems, compared them with Jewish ideas, and modified both to form a new synthesis. But it must not be forgotten that the child is able to fit together his experiences and make sense of them only because of his previous experience of the satisfying coherence of his 'home' ideas. Early Christianity's Jewish background performed this function. A child who has been unable to make sense of the experiences he knows at home, whether it be his literal home or his 'religious' home, will find it difficult to relate later, outside experiences either to each other or to his own experience. He is, typically, disoriented and discontented, finding it hard to concentrate his mind or his energies or carry through any undertaking to its conclusion. It can happen that the parent who is conscientiously trying to protect a child from superstitious ideas may merely succeed in blocking his early attempts to make sense of his environment by means of concepts which are within his reach. It is against this sort of misguided 'enlightenment' that Christ was warning those who thought he had come to destroy the Law. He said he had not come to destroy but to fulfil; that is, to develop the inner meaning and purpose of the Law, to show man how to discover in its fullness what the Law contained germinally. He knew that the ideas that were implicit in his teaching could not yet be taken 'neat', and that the support of a gradually modified version of 'the Law' was and would be essential for a long time. Many of the 'Kingdom' parables show this idea of unfolding, of development, rather than abrupt transition.

Does this mean that parents are justified in teaching children religious concepts which they know to be primitive, distorted by magical interpretation of centuries and morally legalistic? The very idea of an unbelieving parent doing this is obviously absurd, because it is clearly dishonest. The parent would be telling lies, and a lie is still a lie however good the purpose it serves. Moreover, children are terribly quick to detect insincerity. And if a parent who is an unbeliever should not do this, neither, for the same reason, should a Christian. It is just as much a lie for a Christian as for an unbeliever to say 'God is angry with you', however good his intention. Yet some way of talking about the underlying realities of life and love which is not merely negative, or fragmented, needs to be found. It is not enough to deny the magical or mythical links suggested to the child himself by his companions or his books or his own observations. Nor is it enough merely to 'explain' individual phenomena, though this is necessary too. What the

child needs is a comprehensible framework of thought into which
he can fit his experiences, one which can grow with him by
continuing to show new depths as his ability to appreciate them
develops.

Christ used such a framework and his method of teaching the
religiously immature was based on it. Almost always he taught in
stories or parables, and even when he expressed religious ideas
in a form too brief to be called a parable he still used phrases
which were obviously metaphorical. They were satisfyingly
simple to the religiously immature and yet capable of unlimited
development by those whose spiritual perception was greater,
and this without any drastic break or contradiction between forms
of understanding.

That Christ's method was not a personal idiosyncracy but was
due to his understanding of human needs is shown by the fact
that the traditional myths or 'fairy tales' serve the same purpose.
Their significance is greater than mere entertainment at bedtime.
They nourished countless generations of men, giving them a
superficially simple but in reality enormously subtle framework of
symbols into which to fit experience. They can still do this. The
Jewish myths preserved in the Old Testament do the same thing,
and their value is enduring, though for historical reasons they are
virtually useless to the modern unbeliever who has been cut off
from them by the centuries of Christian fundamentalism, whereas
the pagan myths have not suffered this impoverishment in the
name of faith.

The use of stories, similes and myths as a means of spiritual
education involves no kind of intellectual dishonesty. Most
children ask, sometime or other, 'What is God?'. It is not enough
either to deny that there is such a thing as God, or for a believer to give a definition of God which, however apparently
abstract, is inevitably symbolic and in any case totally inadequate.
But even those who must deny the existence of anything that
corresponds to the traditional Christian definitions of the nature
of God are well aware that God exists and has existed, *for
people*, and has been and is an enormously strong influence

in human development. So some sort of answer which is not merely negative is required, an answer which, like all good answers, puts the questioner in touch with a new complex of ideas and so leads to the exploration of new aspects of living. So in this matter Christians and unbelievers are to some extent facing the same problem, and Christ demonstrates the constructive solution for both.

The founder of Christianity was not addicted to theological definitions. Those attributed to him usually have the air of being the evangelist's clarification of Christ's thought for the benefit of his readers. This does not mean that the expression of his thought is inauthentic. It does seem to mean that abstract reflections on matters beyond the reach of the senses are not normally much use as means of establishing immediate contact with people who are 'hungry and thirsty for goodness'. The abstraction may come in useful later, but it is the act of adherence, of trust, that must come first, and to assist this other methods are better. The nearest thing to an abstract definition by Christ of the nature of God to be found in the gospels occurs in that of St John, the most theologically minded of the four, and occurs in the passage already quoted: 'God is spirit, and they that worship him must worship in spirit and in truth.' And as soon as the phrase 'God is spirit' is inserted into its full context it becomes something much richer than a mere definition. The shift of meaning in the two uses of the word 'spirit' immediately shows that the point of the 'spirituality' of God is one of relationship.

The basic relationship between man and God is a spiritual one, one established at the core of human life and not essentially affected by geographical location, which was what was worrying the Samaritan woman in this episode. The 'spirit' was not, to Jewish thought, a separate something that merely 'belonged' to a man. It was a man's complete self, his essential being-in-action. This saying of Christ, even if it was actually spoken by him and was not St John's gloss on his words, means that contact with ('worship' of) God takes place essentially in the very core of a man's existence, and that this is where he touches the existence, the 'spirit', of God. Exterior expressions of this contact, or emotions connected with it, are only ways of making this 'spiritual' encounter easier to apprehend. So even this description of God is not so much a definition of what God is but of how men are related to God, and this is what is expressed in the large number of parables and similes that Christ habitually used in teaching. 'The Kingdom of Heaven' is the 'region' of this contact, and this phrase is itself a kind of double metaphor combining the idea of the powerful influence and immediate relevance to all men of the 'Father' (another metaphor) and the idea of 'otherness', of a different kind of life from that of earthly experience. 'Heaven' or 'sky' was one of several euphemisms used by the Jews for the unnameable God and it carries the emphasis on 'otherness'. But the central theme of the Kingdom of Heaven was explained by means of easily understood illustrations. 'The Kingdom of Heaven is like . . .', 'The Kingdom of Heaven may be compared to . . .': phrases like these introduce the stories or similes. Sometimes the story is told without introduction, in answer to a question, or without one. The hearers are expected to work out for themselves the relevance of the story to the question, spoken or unspoken, that inspired it, and this is a method that especially appeals to children. It is both emotionally and intellectually satisfying, and at the same time it opens wide the doorway to bigger ideas and experiences. It expands mind and heart at once, it really educates, in a way that a merely 'factual' answer can never do, though factual answers have their important place. And whether the story-answers to questions of the 'What is God?' variety are introduced in a form such as 'God is like this' or one such as 'People have thought of God like this' makes, it seems to me, very little difference. In both cases the grown-up is giving the child access to new and important realms of human understanding. The child is not confined either by 'facts' or 'anti-facts'. He is liberated, in the way that Christ himself indicated as proper to a child, by the establishment of a satisfying bond with an idea expressed in comprehensible terms. And this idea contains in itself the means to adventure and discovery by linking experience of self with environment and providing the means of relating each to the other in a potentially limitless development.

Thus a small boy listening to a fairy tale will be drawn to the prince in the story. He will identify himself with the prince, act out his adventures mentally or even physically, feeling the prince's courage, resourcefulness and strength as his own. This will really develop these qualities in him, and he will discover from experience how they apply in the 'real' world. In the same way the image of the Father, King, or Master in Christ's parables works both imaginatively and practically. The relationship between these images of authority and love, and a son or servant, fits the child's emotional knowledge as well as being imaginatively accessible.

The development can certainly continue into adult life without a break. If background and education and innate intelligence limit intellectual curiosity and restrict the flexibility or range of the ideas of which a particular grown-up can make use, the religious ideas imparted in this way will remain comparatively undeveloped and 'childish'. But they will still 'work' as a means of integrating the person with his experiences. This 'working' may, however, be prevented by clumsy attempts to expose the simple symbols of the myths as objectively 'not true' and therefore without value. This is the same as the 'scandalising' of a child, referred to earlier. The result of this fake opposition between what is held to be fact and what is held to be fiction is not enlightenment but radical impoverishment, a spiritual stunting which is tragic, common, and frequently applauded in the name of science, realism, and 'things as they are'.

At this moment in history this all too successful breaking of the link with 'home' is often inflicted on the individual child because it has happened and is happening to the community as a whole. Our civilisation has been assailed by new ideas which it is not spiritually mature enough to relate to earlier thought forms. This premature destruction (rather than encouraged evolution) of myths is not even a service to the science in whose name it is carried out. Science, as a human activity, depends on the ability to synthesise, to reach out from fact to fact and create a new whole, and to go on from these wholes to discover new relationships and still other and greater wholes. The destruction of the myth-patterns of thought inhibits the ability to think in wholes, and therefore discourages scientific thinking. On the other hand the natural development of myth-thinking is by constantly relating the myth to experience and modifying each by the other, as a small child modifies his understanding of his environment by reference to his parents, and vice versa. It does not rule out respect for facts, it fosters it by encouraging a view of facts not just in themselves but as related to each other. An education which took into account the need for a myth framework of *some* kind as an essential condition of human development would not equate knowledge with facts or enlightenment with the premature destruction of illusion.

On the other hand it is desirable that illusions should be shed, provided we can think of illusions not as ideas which are 'not true' but as immature and incomplete expressions of things whose reality it is our business as human beings to pursue. But one illusion, in the popular sense of something 'not true', is that, when one set of illusions (in the other sense) has been successfully shed, what is then received is 'the thing as it is'. Rather what is then seen is a new, more complex and flexible 'illusion', one better related, perhaps, to the elusive reality, but still only a stage on the journey, and providing no excuse for intellectual arrogance or spiritual complacency. The new perception is not necessarily 'more true' it may even be 'less true' in one sense, because the objectivity needed in order to increase knowledge of an idea removes us from the 'centre' which was firmly grasped before, though the grasp was expressed in very simple terms.

A primitive level of religious understanding does not necessarily mean a low level of spiritual achievement. On the contrary, the simple and satisfying intellectual and emotional grasp of religion which belongs to a primitive stage can and observably does make possible a very high degree of personal dedication and goodness, and the development of remarkable spiritual gifts. These things are, temporarily at least, less likely in the stages of new discovery because energy is being deflected into the process of spiritual 'growing up', and the sense of 'oneness', though not necessarily the fact of it, is lessened or even lost.

This is the same process as when the child finds it necessary to separate himself from his parents in order to discover himself and his environment more completely. His relationship with the source of his life becomes, for the time, less immediate and satisfying, he appears to 'love' them less completely. But this is a necessary development, a part of the pursuit of a more ultimately truthful relationship, and to refuse it because of the price that must be paid is to risk losing the thing itself, as in the parable of the talents.

The necessary process of disillusion is not confined to the intellect. That area of consciousness which comes under the heading of 'moral' is inseparably linked to the whole personal development and follows the same stages, though for convenience it is helpful to consider it separately. An arbitrary code of conduct is necessary to the small child, as is a simple framework of thought. This is so because the tiny child has absolutely no 'moral sense' at all, any more than he has any other ideas of his own. In order to be able to classify and cope with the experiences that crowd on him he needs some standard by which to judge them, and this standard is simply the opinion of his parents about what is 'good' and 'bad'. He judges this not only from what they say but from what they do, and may interpret quite accidental events, like a fall, as evidence of his mother's or father's 'anger'. He will then search for some action of his which might have caused this 'anger', and so satisfy his need to discover cause and effect. This is why a consistent code of conduct and consistent behaviour in relation to the child's deeds and misdeeds is so essential to his confidence and ability to adjust himself to his experiences. The fact of some things being good or bad in the sense of pleasant or unpleasant in their effects is not, clearly, something a child has to learn by thinking about it. This he experiences. But in order to come to terms with these experiences he needs to be able to label them, and also to relate them to other events, as in the example just given. This is why a definite, basically reasonable and fairly inflexible moral code is important at the primitive stage of development. It is necessary to be able to label some things as 'sinful' or 'wrong' in order to grow up, rejecting what is 'wrong' with a confidence that could only come from a very clear and uncomplicated concept of 'wrongness'. As St Paul says, 'sin indeed was in the world before the Law was given (as even a baby knows when he is cold or lonely or hungry) but sin is not counted where there is no law'. And again, 'Law came in to increase the trespass', since it is more morally harmful to do something you are certain is wrong than to do something and afterwards discover that it has unpleasant effects. Yet the second alternative means moral chaos and arrested development, because if there is no guide to action except its after-effects the prospect is too frightening to be faced. A child left without any moral guidance will in practice construct some sort of moral code for himself, but the distress and fear and uncertainty he suffers in the process may well distort his future development entirely.

The moral law given to a child by his parents is, to him, quite arbitrary. He doesn't want it to be anything else. It is enough for him that it is the expression of their will, for they are his standard of right and wrong. At this stage there is no 'moral sense' in the usual meaning of the phrase. In a similar way it seems that to the ordinary Israelite before the exile (to generalise monstrously) there was little distinction between the sinfulness of adultery and of an offence of ritual defilement. The Hebrew prophets were gradually developing a more mature attitude to morality, but the ordinary people, including most of the priests, were quite content with a pagan attitude in which the thunderstorm that wrecked a man's crops must be immediately related to some evil action of his preceding it, and the offering of the correct sacrifice wiped out the guilt of sin without reference to the state of mind of the sinner.

The 'letter of the Law' is precious to a developing (not a static) religious community in its early stages as it is to the small child. It really is precious, because it gives the stable frame of reference that is needed, a fixed standard by which to judge the 'morality' of exterior events. As with a theology expressed in myths of some kind or other, this rigid and undiscriminating standard is used as a means of classifying and measuring and making comprehensible the surrounding world. But as the ability to cope with impinging experiences increases, as the variety and quantity of the knowledge of cause and effect is extended, the facts learned are more and more related to each other and form systems which can begin to be related to the original moral systems. Then discrepancies begin to be apparent between ritual 'rightness' and real moral 'wrongness' in the form of hatred or dishonesty or cruelty. A wrong act begins to be distinguished from a wrong intention. 'I didn't mean to' is the child's earliest expression of an understanding that the attitude of the 'heart' matters as much as, if not more than, exterior acts. Or in the words of the prophet quoted by Christ, 'I will have mercy and not sacrifice', and 'these people worship me with their lips but their heart is far from me'.

The balance shifts at this stage from judgment of all exterior manifestations of causality by reference to the arbitrary 'Law of God', to judgment of the details of the 'Law of God' itself by reference to observed and experienced sequences of real cause and effect, especially psychological cause and effect—for instance that kindness ('mercy') makes people happier whereas ritual acts *without* personal involvement do not have any noticeable beneficial effect on the person offering the sacrifice. The virtual annihilation of the Jewish nation and the long exile in Babylon forced the Jews, led by their prophets, to re-interpret radically their attitude to God and their idea of his attitude to them. Henceforward he is a 'moral' God, in our sense. But no sudden complete change in attitude can take place. For some time the child (or the religious community) may try simply to adjust the original 'given' code to the gradually acquired understanding of 'morality' in our sense of the word. If the code that is 'given', in the sense of requiring no validation but itself, is well related to the needs of human beings living in a society it will survive this process very well, and the underlying good sense of its rules will become increasingly apparent as its 'given' character becomes less important. If on the other hand the code, originally functional, no longer serves any clear purpose but has become purely a way of protecting a particular way of life (whether it be Jewish nationhood or a system of class privilege) it will not stand up well to this kind of adjustment, and sooner or later there will be a choice between a total rejection of it (or of those aspects of it which are no longer relevant) and a capitulation to its irrationality for the sake of security. In the latter case no further moral evolution is possible, indeed a stronger and stronger 'fence' of sub-regulations must be devised in order to protect the code which is threatened from outside. Of this kind was, for instance, the incredibly elaborate 'fence round the Law' of minute regulations and interpretations devised by the Rabbis in the centuries immediately before Christ. This code was designed to cover every possible contingency of daily living so that no room was left for judgments and decisions based on any other kind of moral standard than that imposed by the code itself. Christ told these lawyers that by doing this, they had 'taken away the key of knowledge. You would not enter the Kingdom yourselves, and you hindered those who were entering.' Of this kind also are the rules of 'etiquette' which surround a particular social class and protect a code of behaviour (once functional, as in feudalism, but since obsolete as a social system) from judgment by any wider standard.

At the stage of religious development at which Christ 'took over' the Jewish ethos, the process of evolution was already well on, in spite of the tough 'fencing' put up by the Rabbis to protect it from evolution. He roundly condemned this 'fence' but not the Law itself, which provided a true and reasonable and human basis for conduct and was most necessary as a support for the moral evolution of the community as of the individual. On the other hand he did definitely swing the balance right over to a standard of morality which judged primarily by the disposition of the 'heart' rather than by exterior acts, and this was something that particularly annoyed his enemies who saw in it, rightly, a threat to their power over the consciences of the ordinary people.

But he did more than this. With all his emphasis on the need for Law he was offering a notion of morality which implicitly but definitely placed the 'centre' of morality in the individual conscience, but a conscience which was 'of God'. 'He who is of God hears the words of God; the reason why you do not hear them is that you are not of God.' And if I understood rightly the saying that 'God is spirit and those who worship him must worship him in spirit and in truth', then being 'of God' means being 'in touch' with the deepest levels of one's own being, because it is at this level, according to Christ, that contact with God is made, however it may be outwardly assisted in various ways. So the man who is 'in touch' with his essential self is in a position to 'hear the words of God'. In the context of this quotation, Christ was talking about the inability of some of the Pharisees to realise that what he was saying was 'of God', and he offered no proof of the truth of his words except the authentication that should be provided by a man's own heart if he is 'of God'. Obviously, being 'of God' in this sense is not something that happens automatically; it is the end of a long process of spiritual evolution by way of 'the Law'. And the fact that Christ demanded this kind of spiritual sensitivity of these men who were experts in the Law shows that he conceived of the Law as leading naturally, if properly developed ('fulfilled'), to the state of being able to judge for oneself what is 'of God'—that is, in accordance with the deepest needs and desires of human life. The Lawyer who asked 'Who is my neighbour?' showed this by the rightness of his moral judgment on the story of the good Samaritan. In the story, the 'right' behaviour according to the Law, literally interpreted, was to 'pass by on the other side' in order to avoid ritual defilement. The Lawyer realised that this was less important than the 'rightness' of the gesture of compassion. This was his moment of revelation, when he recognised a moral criterion in his own heart (a heart formed by the Law if ever one was) and was prepared to commit himself to it openly. He had 'heard the words of God' because he was 'of God'.

Myth and Law are the two 'parents' of the human spirit. By 'loving' them and growing in and by them the child, whether it be an individual child or a human community, grows and becomes able to accept and adapt to its environment. It must develop and adventure and break free from both parents, but in order to do so it must still preserve the bond of love, the 'state of belief' that unites it to its parents, and supports its adventures and questionings. This bond must be rediscovered and renewed in a new form at every stage, but if it be broken, development is distorted or prevented unless a substitute can be found. The renewal of the bond becomes, after a while, a free, willed act, and this is the act of 'becoming like little children' that Christ demanded of his followers as a condition of discovering his Kingdom.

CHAPTER III

'WHAT GOD HAS JOINED'

Relationships as self-discovery

In Chapter I, we examined the first condition of progress towards human maturity: a desire for it. In chapter II it was necessary to study the conditions for the successful beginning of development, according to this desire, towards 'the Kingdom of Heaven', which means the completeness of being human. This beginning depends on a good relationship between the child and his parents. Similar progress in the community depends on a satisfying relationship between the community and its gods, whatever they may be. From the very beginning, then, human development depends on good relationships.

But the need for relationship is even more fundamental than this implies.

People who are incarcerated in darkness and solitude for any length of time rapidly lose all sense of time, of any kind of relation with external reality. Eventually they lose even the desire to eat, for the fundamental instinct of self-preservation is destroyed also. They begin to disintegrate as human beings. This has been demonstrated by volunteers in recent experiments, and it has been recorded by concentration camp survivors.

It has been noticed by doctors and social workers that babies in some institutions, reared without the stimulation of normal human love and contact—though properly fed and washed—remain mentally and psychologically inert, uninterested, unsmiling, inactive lumps of humanity. This shows, in an acute form, something of which we are all aware, though generally without thinking about it—the fact that no human being can discover himself, become conscious of himself, except in relation to other human beings. Human growth consists of the working out of human relationships, and a man who can subsist entirely without human contacts can only do so either if he has managed to create for himself an emotional substitute for human relationship or has already reached a stage of considerable spiritual maturity and self-knowledge.

If this is true it means that any kind of deeper understanding of the meaning of being human will come about by the enlargement of the knowledge of what relations between human beings are, and how they work.

This may seem so obvious as to be hardly worth saying. But its obviousness is the obviousness of everyday living, and tends to be disregarded when the pursuit of truth, or ultimate meaning, or a unifying principle, or other high-sounding aims are being discussed. Yet any true understanding of human living cannot be one developed by the intellect and imposed on the behaviour of ordinary life from outside. It must grow out of the experience of living, with the intellect comparing and judging and directing further stages, a working together of thought and feeling and physical activity. And the experience of living is the experience of relationships, of 'being for'. All insight into the meaning or even existence of a 'self' comes from the experience of the self in relation. But in order to be a development, and not just a succession of isolated experiences, there must be the act of faith, the explicit or implicit commitment to search for something as yet unknown.

This is why the teaching of Christ not only stresses the necessity of search for the Kingdom of Heaven but makes it equally clear that the area of the search, wherever else it may be, is primarily that of relations between people. It is the opposite of those philosophies which stress detachment from human contacts and desires. In Christ's view there is to be no withdrawal into communion with the source of life if that means withdrawal from people; in fact he makes ordinary, concrete, down-to-earth usefulness to other people the test of the reality of any man's search for truth. Professions of devotion to himself which do not issue in devotion to other people are empty and useless. To disciples who cry 'Lord! Lord!' he pictures himself replying 'I do not know you'.

They are using his name to make themselves important, to claim a privileged position. But they did not do 'the will of my Father', they refused to serve men, and therefore cut themselves off from Christ.

But, in his mind, 'works' however remarkable are not in themselves necessarily 'the will of my Father'. In many places he makes it clear that, odd as it may seem, the first condition of doing 'the works of God' is to 'believe in the one whom he has sent'. This 'believing', this faith whose necessity Christ was never tired of emphasising, seems to be precisely that attitude of commitment to a search which 'enlightens' a man *in relation to other men*. By it he can 'see' them, not as objects on which to exercise his gifts and virtues to his own aggrandisement ('did we not cast out devils in your name?' protest the self-important disciples in the story, shut out of their master's house) but as beings whose value is Christ's own value as his Father's representative: 'If you did it to the least of my brothers you did it to me.' If *other people* are the way to the truth, to self-discovery and the Kingdom of Heaven, then all that separates man from man is an obstacle to being properly human. 'The blind see, the deaf hear, the lame walk, the dead are raised, and the poor have the good news proclaimed to them.' These are the proofs or 'signs' of the validity of his mission which Christ offered to his cousin John. The inclusion of the last clause is especially significant because it shows at once that the relief of physical suffering was, in Christ's eyes, only a way of making it possible for men to hear 'the good news' he had come to preach, the good news of his Kingdom. On many occasions he made it clear that both physical relief and the release from a burden of guilt were necessary in order to make way for the Kingdom of Heaven and he coupled forgiveness and healing in a way which seems odd to modern ideas. Yet he did not, as his contemporaries did, couple sin and sickness as simple cause and effect; in fact he explicitly rejected this view, though he showed himself aware of a connection of a more complex kind such as is being re-discovered by modern medical science. To him, both sickness and sin were incompatible with the Kingdom of Heaven, because both these evils cut off a man from other men. The lepers, cut off entirely from the community, are an extreme example and symbol of this, and Christ showed his understanding of the real root of their suffering when he healed them by touching them, which was something no one else would do. This symbol of oneness was his normal gesture of both mental and physical healing.

In the mind of Christ, this refusal to accept any kind of barrier must be carried, if necessary, to apparently lunatic extremes, as in the famous saying about 'turning the other cheek'. Anything in the way of personal suffering is preferable to the erection of such barriers against the other person as must be created by reacting to attack with retaliation, sulks, or fantasies of revenge. 'Turning the other cheek' cannot abolish the other's hatred, but it can make it clear that there is no further barrier, and thereby make it easier to lower the existing one.

So this abolishing of barriers is the essential means to the establishment of the Kingdom of Heaven.

Christ's work in this, as he described it, is to be the light that shows up the 'Kingdom', the lovableness in each man, and makes it seem worthwhile to overcome the obstacles; and, when necessary for the same end, he is the 'shepherd' who brings back the stray into the life of the flock. But this destruction of barriers is not merely negative, it is the preparation for a much more fundamental kind of relationship, a new kind of life altogether, one proper to the Kingdom.

This new life is in fact the thing we call 'love,' in its Christian interpretation, which is very clear but not very easy to define. The nature of the Christian notion of love will appear more fully as it is used in various contexts, but as a working definition it can be described as the act of the spirit, the essential self of man, in its desire to remove barriers and communicate fully. Love is that which searches, in the fullest sense, and gives and desires.

St Paul compares Christ's love for the people of God (which, as Christ made clear, was potentially every man) with the love of a husband for his wife, 'as Christ loved the Church and gave himself up for her'. The Church, the People of God, is not some abstract thing, but simply people. It was to people that Christ wanted to reveal a new quality of love so as to make them able to love in this way. It was this love for and between people—ordinary, sinful people—that St Paul compares to the love of husband and wife at its best. But the idea conveyed by the phrase 'he gave himself up for her' is far deeper and more far-reaching than any idea of marriage that was current at the time when this was written. St Paul's estimate of the reality of marriage as he saw it around him is not flattering, and indeed it is difficult to see at first why he should have chosen an institution so obviously bound to material interests as marriage appeared to be, as an image of the highest and most complete kind of love imaginable.

But the image of sexual love was not a new one in the development of Jewish theology. The Jewish prophets had been accustomed to speak of God's relations with Israel in terms of a husband and wife relationship. Hosea talked of Israel as the erring and adulterous wife who may perhaps be punished, but is always loved, pursued and forgiven. He could picture the Lord as completely ignoring the unfaithfulness of his beloved. 'Therefore, behold, I will allure her, and bring her into the wilderness, and speak tenderly to her.' 'I will betroth you to me in righteousness and in justice, in steadfast love and in mercy. I will betroth you to me in faithfulness, and you shall know the Lord.' All this, after behaviour on the part of God's people which he and the other prophets described in terms of prostitution on a grand scale, and in outspoken language which made large portions of Scripture forbidden reading for the young in respectable families of past generations.

It is this kind of love which St Paul says Christ has for the Church (that is, for each human being) and he, also, compares it to the love of husband for wife. And it is to precisely this kind of love that Christ himself summoned his followers. 'Love one another, as I have loved you.' If the love for each other that is demanded of those who take Christ for their guide is of a kind that can properly be compared to sexual love, then this says something both about sexual love and about the quality of inter-personal love which is proper to the Kingdom of Heaven—that is, the full development of what is implied in being human. It is therefore vital to an understanding of Christ's ideas about love to understand what is implied by the ideal and why there seems to have been, even until now, so large a gap between this ideal and the attitude to actual marriages in the Christian tradition.

First it is as well to be clear that the kind of love that St Paul used as a comparison was specifically sexual love, and not just love in a married relationship, which in its human expression includes sex. The passage in the book of Genesis to which Christ referred in his own remarks about marriage described how God provided man with a mate 'of his own kind' because 'it is not good for man to be alone'. (This might quite legitimately be paraphrased as: 'It is not according to man's proper nature for him to live in isolation, he can only develop properly through relationship.') 'And this is why a man leaves his father and mother and cleaves to his wife, and they become one single body.' Therefore, Christ comments, 'What God has joined it is not for men to part.' But St Paul quotes this Genesis definition, the 'two in one flesh' or 'one single body', when he is denouncing intercourse with prostitutes. His reason for forbidding it is that this physical union makes the Christian, who is 'one with Christ', 'one body' with the prostitute. To him, then, the basic significance of sexual union is the same for good or for ill, in a lifelong partnership or a casual liaison. When St Paul talks of the union of Christ with the People of God he is thinking in terms of a union which is essentially loving, but he does not compare it to just *any* kind of unselfish 'devoted' (in the biblical sense which is one of ruthless, uncompromising dedication) love, but specifically to devoted *sexual* love with the same 'becoming one body' significance that belongs to sexual union in any form, however degraded.

It looks as if there is something about sexual union as such which is basic to the understanding of Christ's concept of the Kingdom of Heaven, or 'eternal life', two phrases which are ways of describing the ultimate fulfilment of being human. This is not as odd as it sounds if one considers the age-long tendency to see in sexual intercourse the link between the world of temporal human activity and the 'other' world of the gods, of the mysterious forces beyond man's understanding that control the universe. Ritual prostitution as a means of harnessing divine fertility could and did become superstitious and grossly commercialised. But the idea behind it is one that persists and has had a renaissance recently in the quasi-mystical cult of sex as the *summum bonum*. Although the Jewish tradition violently rejected this expression of the idea, with all that it implied of a limitation of the divinity, it also enshrined the idea itself in the bridal metaphor beloved of Jewish prophetic writers and their successors in the Christian tradition.

Nor is it so odd, from a different point of view, if one considers Christ's idea that it is of the nature of his Kingdom both to require and bring about the destruction of barriers between people, that healing and the forgiveness of sin were part of the removal of such barriers, and that the normal sign of both healing and forgiveness was immediate physical contact. The idea, whether consciously understood or not, has been preserved in the sacramental rites of the Christian tradition in which outward gestures of physical touching are used as signs.

These things taken together seem to show that Christ's idea of the love that belongs to his Kingdom is not ideally expressed simply in 'doing things for other people' though 'doing things' is the practical test of its sincerity. It is a love that aims at complete union by the abolition of all that separates, and the acts of practical service have this end and this end only. Any other purpose makes them irrelevant to ('shut out' from) his Kingdom. And although some of his sayings make clear that his idea of the final development of human living will not involve marriage in any sense that is meaningful to us it is also clear that, as an essential stage on the way to the unimaginable end, the physical expression of love, of which sexual intercourse is the most complete example, is essential. The 'one body' of sexual union is in some sense the ideal, but only when it is the expression of a complete 'self-giving'. Actual human sexual union should, in the light of this teaching, properly be one of complete self-giving, and it also carries the implication of a sort of finality that belongs to it by nature (what God has joined) though this can, of course, be ignored. But it also follows that every kind of inter-human act is in some way related to the self-giving act of sexual love and should express this relation. This is a simple and, once perceived, rather obvious deduction from the words attributed to Christ (whether he uttered them or not is irrelevant in one sense, since in any case the early Church held them to be an essential part of his message) and from the use of the symbol of sexual union by St Paul.

But the idea of sexual love has had to go through the same process of historical development as the wider notion of morality of which, in fact, it forms the pivot. And, as with morality in general, Christ's ideas about it came at the point where 'the Law' had developed understanding to a level at which a new concept 'in spirit and in truth' could begin to take root but could not possibly be expected to show full development, let alone a final form.

So, inevitably and rightly, his ideas were interpreted in terms of 'the Law' and so carried and made available through the centuries, 'working' even when their conscious expression was legalistic, until a stage of understanding should be reached at which the balance may safely shift decisively from an exterior norm (the Law) to an interior understanding of the meaning of humanness as learned by the assistance of the Law. The development of ideas about the meaning of sex during the Christian era has shaped our whole culture. Therefore an understanding of the development of the forms that shaped it is essential to an understanding of the meaning of sex in human life as we see it now.

The history of Christian phobias about sex, their origins (essentially non-Christian), the long drawn-out struggle to integrate them into Christianity and then to change and eventually to discard them is fascinating if rather revolting. It follows a pattern familiar in individual development, by which ideas imposed by environment become so embedded that they seem to be an essential part of a person, and are understood and explained as such. If the personality has sufficient strength and vitality it can modify these ideas, and the behaviour associated with them, by comparing them with other ideas it encounters, and eventually it may be able to discard them altogether, though this usually requires a crisis of some kind, an obvious and inescapable challenge and choice. Not all of the body of ideas absorbed in the formative period are necessarily discarded, though they may appear to be if the form in which they have habitually been expressed is too closely identified with the discarded system. The elements that are kept, if any, are naturally those that 'fit' the person and help his proper development, so much so that he may easily not realise that they have been learned from the system of thought now rejected as fake or at least inadequate. The recognition of what is good in a discarded system or its recognition as in fact derived from that system is more likely if there is affection and trust for the source of it, whether it be the parents or some religious or social community. This is the process I discussed earlier in relation to the change from development within the framework of the Law to that depending on 'spirit and truth', the interior understanding of the person himself. The development of sexual ethics in the Christian era is part of this line of development, but it is given a special twist, the reasons for which are not at first obvious, by a significant combination of outward circumstances and inward needs.

At the risk of over-simplifying the complex interaction of historical cause and effect it is worth seeing whether this development makes sense in terms of human self-discovery in the community, as it does in the individual.

The early Christian Church took over a ready-made system of sexual morality from Judaism, and at first took it for granted and indeed did not give it much thought, since the final establishment of Christ's Kingdom was expected at an early date and the working out of long-term human relationships did not seem relevant to a community intent on preparations for an immediate cataclysm. St Paul's reasons for questioning the suitability of the married state for Christians seem to have been connected with this. He never suggested that marriage, or sex in marriage, was in any way wrong, in fact he discouraged couples who had caught such an idea from various philosophies, and told them not to 'deny each other' except perhaps for a short time, by mutual consent and for the purpose of prayer. He denounced sexual licence, and especially promiscuous homosexuality, and the reasons he gives are interesting. Such habits arose, he said, because men 'suppress the truth'. 'They became futile in their thinking and their senseless minds were darkened.' They lost, in fact, the 'light' by which they might continue to search for the truth, and *therefore* 'God gave them up to the lusts of their hearts', for these 'lusts' were their way of trying to escape from the 'darkness' and 'futility' of a life from which the commitment to search was absent. This explanation shows that in the mind of St Paul the shift of moral balance was already made. He does not condemn this kind of behaviour simply in terms of an absolute Law which it transgresses but discovers a reason for the wrongness in a loss of something which is essential to real human development—the search for truth. The sense of direction is lost, and with it a sense of love, but this is two ways of saying the same thing since, as Simone Weil said, 'love is a direction and not a state of the soul'.

But the sanity and honesty of St Paul's mind could not drag the whole community in its progress. Inevitably his teaching, like his Master's, was studied and taught largely in terms of the Law, and in so far as this was the only way it could 'work' for the vast majority this was not only inevitable but right. There were brilliant exceptions, men who saw further by the light of Christ than others. But each one would only cast the light in one direction; for the rest they accepted Christianity as Law, though clearly a more human and inspiring and flexible Law than the rigid Jewish one.

If the Jewish inheritance, which might correspond to that of the parents of a child, had been the only influence on the young community the development could have been comparatively simple, though perhaps not very spectacular. In fact there were other influences at work from the beginning, and though they were diverse they were all of the kind that expresses, from time to time, the almost overpowering desire to break out of the human condition as it is experienced. Such ideas come out strongly at times when the social or religious order has become too tidy and practical to be humanly tolerable, and the Roman Empire presented such an atmosphere to perfection. 'A place for everything and everything in its place' sums up fairly well the Roman ideal, and the human spirit, thus tidied up, organised and classified, found no place had been left for it to grow. Attempts to break out took the form, as usual, of a nose-dive into the subconscious, an occupation that was necessarily confined to initiates who had undergone a rigorous process of separation from adherence to conscious and material concerns. The variety and incredible complexity of the gnostic doctrines, pursuing exclusive sub-conscious enlightenment by all sorts of symbolic elaborations, is amazing, but all of them had in common a distrust and indeed a hatred of the material world and especially of sex.

It is not relevant here to go into the various forms in which the fear and hatred of sex was embodied in gnostic teaching and symbolism. The point is that the gnostic influence was so strong that although it was explicitly and furiously rejected by the Church it did, as often happens, shape the unconscious attitudes of Christians, so that they ended by explaining Christian ideas in ways that were compatible with the gnostic mentality, particularly where sex was concerned. The same pressures that bred gnosticism were, after all, affecting everybody, including the members of the Christian community, so this result is not very surprising.

The Christian emotional (though seldom theological) equation of sex and sin was reinforced by the combination of two other factors. One was the Judaic condemnation of extra-marital sexuality. This condemnation may be attributed at least in part to the fact that the Jewish sense of purpose in history was embodied in the destiny of the nation as a whole, and the sense of 'belonging' which was essential to the preservation of this purposefulness in times of exile, foreign influence, or national disaster depended on each male Jew 'belonging' securely and absolutely to the nation through the stable succession of the generations of his family.

Extra-marital sexuality, but more particularly the unspeakable crime of intercourse with a foreigner, could weaken this feeling of belonging and 'dilute' the sense of vocation and purpose in a tiny nation that had no security of land, riches, or armed might to bolster up its confidence in itself and its mission.

The other factor belonged to the Gentile world into which Christianity emerged so rapidly. This was the sexual 'division of labour': wives were for breeding, but not normally for pleasure which—including intellectual pleasure—was provided by male lovers or by hetarae. Combining these two systems of thought, it was easy enough to equate sexual pleasure with extra-marital sexuality and therefore, by comparing it with the inherited Jewish code, with sin. If the only permissible kind of sexual activity was within marriage then its purpose must be purely procreative and any other was of the devil. This is miles away from the rationally balanced arguments of St Paul, but it was a view that became almost universal among Christians, and we find many of the early Fathers (Tertullian for instance) becoming quite hysterical in denunciations of the power of woman to drag a man down to animal level by sexual allurement.

These ideas continued unabated through the centuries, and although the Church steadfastly repudiated the gnostic notion that sexual intercourse in marriage was essentially sinful it was easily accepted that intercourse for pleasure (without the intention of procreation) was likely to be 'venially sinful'. Married couples were also urged to avoid intercourse for periods varying from a day to a fortnight before receiving the Eucharist. The Catharist form of gnosticism was rejected, with struggles whose bitterness scarred the Church for centuries to come, but the courtly or romantic ideal which appears to have grown out of the heresy exalted sexual love but tended to despise sexual intercourse as unworthy of so refined a passion. In any case it placed the highest form of love between the sexes firmly outside marriage. So the romantic tradition, even within the orthodox faith, perpetuated a denigration of marriage.

All this fear and suspicion of sex naturally tended to the

exaltation of virginity, first simply because it avoided sex and then as a positive value in itself, an assertion of the primacy of the spirit over the evil flesh. St Paul's (and apparently Christ's) recommendations to virginity were 'for the Kingdom of Heaven's sake', that is as a means by which some Christians could more easily carry on that searching and loving to which they were called by the service of the Kingdom, and in certain kinds of work especially. The mystique of virginity which grew up was supported by an interpretation of St Paul's writings in which his special (originally Jewish but very personal) use of the terms 'the flesh' and 'the spirit' was ignored in favour of a simple dualistic understanding—'the flesh', meaning the body and especially sex, and 'the spirit', meaning un-physical or 'spiritual' activities, a reading which would have made St Paul, with his Jewish feeling for the wholeness of a human being, tear his hair.

But even if it is possible now to see how all this happened, and to reject these ideas as a fantastic distortion of common-sense and experience, of human aspirations and of the teaching of the gospel, it should also be possible to look back and see whether these ideas have contributed something essential and valuable to the development of the understanding of the human person and human love, without which we should be the poorer. It may be that the idea of virginity, which seems to be negative, an arbitrary barrier, is in fact a means to the development of properly human relationship.

The ideal of virginity was given a positive significance in the Christian mystique which it had never had before. Repudiation of sex has never been uncommon among people dedicated to spiritual pursuits, whether religious or philosophical, but the Christian renunciation, though as utilitarian as any of these in its beginnings and in its prejudices, took on an aura of special and positive holiness. The virgin was betrothed to Christ, and the language used to describe the relationship, from very early days until now, has been frankly and unashamedly sexual. But recently a Catholic theologian wrote that 'baptism makes us virgins, by taking us out of the carnal (i.e. 'of the flesh' in the Pauline, not the normal sense) world and raising us in the Spirit . . . the Church is made a virgin in her union with her Saviour's sacred body'.[1] Such ideas have echoed down the Christian centuries, and they mean a lot more than their literal translation into a career involving actual physical virginity. They mean that the commitment to love, to 'go out' on the search for humanness to which Christ summoned men (remembering that 'love is a direction . . .') means discovering the self in love and by love. But first there must be confidence, security, the child's awareness of himself as loved, holy, whole. Only this can make possible the union with Christ which, according to him, is expressed by unlimited self-giving to other people. The ideal of Christian virginity means the realisation of oneself as loved by Christ. Only a person who had such an assurance of his own self-hood, of the dignity of being lovable, is capable of the courage and adventurousness required for the search for the Kingdom of Heaven. The same writer says, 'Virginity liberates, but it mainly does so in the depths of the soul [as opposed to practical liberation for some work for which celibacy is obviously desirable]: it liberates love.'

This sense of the essential lovableness of being human seems to have been an entirely new phenomenon. It was one of the central Christian ideas and it certainly did liberate. If it did not always lead to the freeing of slaves (though it often did) it led, when practised by sincere Christians, to their treatment as human beings of equal value with their masters. Their baptism, which was the sign that they were loved by Christ, gave them this value. A good example of this occurs in St Paul's letter to Philemon, about a runaway slave whom Paul had baptised. He sent him back with this message: '. . . he was parted from you for a while, that you might have him back forever, no longer as a slave . . . as a beloved brother, especially to me but how much more to you . . . receive him as you would receive me.'

This conviction of the lovableness of a human being redeemed by Christ has been hideously and constantly obscured, but wherever it has been translated into practice the effect has been the same,

[1] Durrwell, *In the Redeeming Christ*, Sheed and Ward, London, 1964.

for the security of being loved does lead to the liberation of love. The literal and practical application of this idea of wholeness to a state in life has been obscured by being mixed with the negative motive for embracing physical virginity—the fear of and revulsion from sex. But this motive could be reduced to a largely formal acceptance of a current attitude of mind. It seems that it often was reduced to this in the minds and careers of actual people, those who caught the light of the gospel most clearly in spite of their inevitable conditioning by the religious ideas of their time. They responded to the gospel message by adopting the religious, virginal state, and in such cases the ideal of wholeness and lovableness was fully translated into the terms of the state of virginity. It did liberate love, and to know this it is only necessary to read the lives of people like St Gertrude, St Francis, St Teresa, St John Bosco, and hundreds of others whose names are known, not to mention all the unknown monks, friars and nuns whose real human glory is not obscured by the distortions, morbidities and fears of many in the same state of life, nor even by their own incidental oddities and obsessions.

So if the ugly sex-phobia of the Christian tradition has naturally produced some very ugly results it has also helped to isolate and clarify the special Christian sense of individual lovableness. It seems unlikely that this could have been grasped so fully and clearly without its embodiment in a state of life. It is arguable that a time could come when the inner conviction of the personal lovableness of each one could be so clear and unmistakable in the minds of human beings that its manifestation in an actual state of life would no longer be necessary, except when a particular type of work for other people demanded it. But however that may be the ideal of virginity has contributed something which should not be discarded just because it has been too much mixed up with distrust of sex. The good thing that was discovered by the dubious aid of anti-sex prejudices is still there to be used by those who are not inclined to throw out the baby with the bathwater.

For this sense of personal value is not a mere statement that people are worthy of love. Christianity asserts this in the face of philosophies and religions that value human beings solely for their functions. This functional valuation is precisely what has degraded relations between the sexes (whether for breeding or for pleasure), made possible the acceptance of slavery, the concept of 'subject races' and other obvious results of treating human beings as means. So, odd as it may seem, it does look as if the full valuation of sexual relationships as relationships between persons could emerge only on the other side of the glorification of virginity, or at least of the attitude to the individual which it embodied. And before going on to study in detail the human and Christian implications of sexual love, St Paul's words seem to pull these threads together neatly enough: 'I appeal to you therefore, brethren, because of the goodness of God (the love that gives value?) to present your bodies as a living offering, holy and acceptable (whole and lovable) to God, which is your spiritual worship (i.e. communication in depth). Do not be conformed to the age (the age he has described as futile and darkened) but be transformed by the renewal of your minds, that you may prove (find out) what is the will of God (Christ's Kingdom of Heaven), what is good and acceptable and perfect.'

Reading this it seems incredible that St Paul should ever have been thought of as an enemy of the body. If this passage means anything at all in the context of Christ's teaching on love and St Paul's own interpretation of it, it means that it is by a proper valuation of the body for the purposes of love that we shall avoid the futilities and waste of a darkened age and discover what is the 'good and acceptable and perfect' state of human nature. 'What God has joined' is one human spirit to another, and the body is the essential and only means to bring about a spiritual unity, so that men 'on love revealed may look' as John Donne, the major prophet of sexual love, saw very clearly.

CHAPTER IV

'TWO IN ONE FLESH'

The breakthrough of passion

THE search for human goodness implies the desire for some kind of 'liberation' from the human condition that St Paul calls 'the flesh', and this liberation, according to the Christian notion, is essentially one to be achieved in relationship. The way to freedom as described by Christ is by way of human relationship of a particular kind which he characterises by saying that it 'illuminates'— that is, it reveals the truth about a person; that it is 'of the spirit', meaning that it is not just a matter of custom, or of utility in a political or physical sense, but is of the essence of being human; and also that it manifests itself in practical action for the good of others, not merely in interior disposition, or self-knowledge for its own sake.

Any Christian attempt to explore the psychological meaning of sexual love must be defined by this concept of the characteristic quality of human development towards fulfilment. How does sexuality serve this 'illumination' of human life, this development of 'the spirit'?

As soon as the idea of a sexual relationship is considered at all, one obvious link between the experience of sex and the desire for the Kingdom of Heaven leaps to mind. This is the phenomenon known as 'falling in love', sex as passion. As with the ambiguous word 'love', it is necessary first to define 'passion', but the full meaning of the word in the context of human development towards its perfection will become more apparent with use. By 'passion' I do not mean simply the free play of 'instinct' or 'lust' (according to one's point of view). Passion can be quite independent of sexual desire as such, and a whole range of sexual behaviour is possible without passion. Passion as an experience is the drive of a powerful emotion towards the knowledge, and, in some sense, possession, of an object outside oneself. (Denis de Rougemont's use of the word 'passion' in his turning-point book, *Passion and Society*, is very near to mine, but he draws from it implications which I cannot regard as altogether justified.) This chapter is an examination of the nature, working and human significance of the experience of passion in the light of Christ's teaching.

Passion is an experience which has been recognised throughout history and in all kinds of cultures as an event in human life which is both powerful and mysterious. Many cultures have regarded it with suspicion as a socially disintegrating force, and they have some reason on their side.

The medieval Church disapproved of passion because the whole Christian life was seen in terms of the successful application of the law of God, and this law was thought of in terms of statute law, an unchanging principle to be applied in all cases with as much consistency and fairness as possible. But passion is essentially lawless. Sexual passion, as opposed to sex as a gratification of physical desire, or as procreative, brings a sense of liberation from ordinary obligations, opinions and loyalties. It creates in the lover a consuming longing which extends beyond the person of the beloved. It is, as a matter of experience, a new and 'other' life, and the romantic tradition strictly so called, which saw death as the fitting climax of romantic love, was expressing symbolically the fact that passion looks to, and feels assurance of obtaining, something beyond the possibilities of ordinary living. But the carefully wrought achievement of civilisation is very vulnerable. It can only survive so long as those elements of a society which do not benefit from it are prevented in some way from taking action to alter their condition, and this applies not only to those sections of society (slaves, slave races, or the 'lower orders') who can be bullied or bamboozled into accepting their condition as inevitable but also to those parts of human nature itself, even in the persons of the fortunate ones who benefit from civilisation, for which no provision is made in the external organisation of society.

If highly civilised cultures (such as that of classical Greece and eighteenth century Europe) are intolerant of passion but character-ised by a high degree of sexual permissiveness this is because sex, whatever form it takes, is not disruptive of the well-organised person or state, provided it is kept to the level of physical gratifica-tion or pure reproduction and not allowed to affect public be-haviour. It provides a useful outlet for the 'lower appetites' which are kept as much separated from the life of the enlightened mind and emotions as the 'lower orders' are separated from the life of 'society'. (The peculiar sense which we give to the word 'society' in this context was the result of exactly such a need to protect a form of civilisation from disruptive influences.)

Sex as an influence in human life is neither dangerous nor powerful unless the purely physical aspect of it is combined with other aspects of life. The man who is married and who keeps a mistress while preserving a decent silence about it is no threat to society. The necessary psychological separation involved in such an arrangement prevents him from combining the side of his life connected with sex as pleasure with the kind of thoughts and ideas which he regards as part of his 'serious' life as a responsible citizen, and as husband and father. He may be an excellent man, and by means of this double life he may avoid many tensions which might affect his family adversely. Precisely. The separating of sex from 'serious' living makes sex harmless. It is a threat neither to his own peace of mind nor to the stability of the social order,

Francis Bacon, that astute careerist, summed up the opinion of most sensible people about the proper place of 'love': 'They do best who if they cannot but admit love, yet make it keep quarter, and sever it wholly from their serious affairs and actions of life; for if it check once with business it troubleth men's fortunes, and maketh men that they can noways be true to their own ends.' And Dorothy Sayers makes one of her characters observe (in a novel whose plot turns on this psychological fact) that 'Passion's a good, stupid horse that will pull the plough six days of the week, if you give him the run of his heels on Sundays. But love's a nervous, awkward, overmastering brute; if you can't rein him, it's best to have no truck with him.' (Here 'passion' is used to mean 'sex' as I have used the word here. I use 'passion' in a sense near to de Rougemont's special one, of the drive towards the unknown and desired. Miss Sayer's use of 'love' is in fact nearer to this meaning of 'passion', and when sex becomes passion in this sense it is a different matter altogether.)

The Greeks described passion as 'madness' and the eighteenth century either outlawed it as vulgar and ridiculous or tried to tame it into a domestic pet. But this attempt was a forlorn hope. The romantic movement, that expression in literary and artistic terms of the sense of psychological claustrophobia which civilisation inflicts on the more sensitive and honest, could only temporarily be contented with such mild outlets as landscape gardening, the cult of the picturesque and rural, or political radicalism. 'Enthusiasm' is a word for passion in its public form, and it is anathema to the ordered society or to the orderly mind. Plato, who began as a poet, ended by recommending fathers whose sons showed poetic tendencies to use extreme measures to suppress a thing so dangerous to the rule of reason and order. This is logical, for poetry is one means by which the unorganised elements in human nature express themselves. It is not poetry itself which is dangerous—like sex, it can be tamed. The danger is from the 'un-clubbable' delinquents in the psychological organism who make use of it: 'enthusiasm' in society, passion in the individual.

Nowadays there is a large class of young people to whom poetry in the ordinary sense is meaningless, but whose 'unorganised' side is no longer controlled by the sheer fatigue of endless physical labour as was that of their forefathers. They find the equivalent of what was once supplied by poets or preachers in the music of 'pop' singers. The behaviour of pop fans is neither surprising nor shocking once the meaning of passion is understood.

But, as always, the violence or aberrations of passion produce a reaction in certain people, and the modern form of the distrust of passion is very widespread and persuasive. It is not only the prudish and conventional who distrust the evidence of passion. It is possible to regard passion as only artificially combined with sex, which is 'purer' when it remains at the unpretentious level of physical satisfaction. This is the criticism implied by Doctor Comfort, who seems to regard passion as the result of the frustration of 'natural' sex. It appears to him to be a perversion of normal sexuality, which should be given reasonably free rein as a sport, a shared pleasure, an expression of mutual affection, and no more. This is understandable if the 'more' does spring inevitably and only from some form of frustration. It seems reasonable, in that case, to hope for a society in which frustration, and therefore the impulse of passion, would not occur, and human beings could be what they sometimes think they would like to be: contented, rational animals.

At the end of that absorbing but claustrophobic book, *Sex and Society*, Doctor Comfort sums up his idea of the possible future society in which 'contraception and a loss of anxiety over sexual matters generally may mean that erotic interests, which are after all the most psychologically appropriate source of "kicks", will replace not only the adventitious excitements we now pursue, but a fair part of individualistic art and the whole of residual religion, as well, perhaps, as a large part of the "drive" behind modern technological progress . . . permissive societies are not as a rule very original or progressive; our sons and daughters may be willing to accept this for a few generations at least in exchange for the advantages of not being hell-bent on anything. *Even the emotional relationships in such a society might look shallow to us* but our intensity, mirrored in plays and fiction, will look as irrelevant to them as King Oedipus's overreaction to a pardonable mistake. A less intense world might, indeed, be no bad thing.' (My italics.) Later he says, 'The good life, as Bertrand Russell has said, is inspired by love and directed by intelligence. There is no field in which this is more true than in our sexual relationships.' But since he never defines 'love' this hopeful statement gets us little further. Love is not a simple thing to define, and the tacit attempt to exclude the phenomenon of passion from the concept of love really begs the question. The Comfort concept of normal sexuality demands a deliberate simplification of ideas about the human condition. It demands that we rule out the idea of 'maturity' as a possible ideal in human life, except in the sense (a common one) of the achievement of a balance of forces similar to the one we call civilisation when applied to a community. This kind of maturity gives every appearance of being a satisfactory means of living in the world as we know it, and it certainly is no mean achievement. But it involves, necessarily, the construction of a system of interior defences against forces within and without which might upset the balance. The most certain upsetter of the balance, the destroyer of this achieved contentment, is passion.

If that were all it would be reasonable to demand the unconditional suppression of passion, and this is done often enough, either by attempting actual suppression or by describing it as a pardonable folly that will be outgrown, and thereby drawing the teeth of its seriousness. Passion is serious, and takes itself seriously, though the passionate man may laugh at himself for those ways in which he sees his passion to be incongruous with other aspects of himself. But it is a matter of experience that when the defences built up over a period of years for the sake of personal sanity and contented daily living are really threatened by the disruptive force of passion, in whatever form, it is not possible simply to reject it and go on as before. This may be what is desired, this may be what a person thinks he has done, but it does not, and cannot, happen. When the threat is a real one either the defences must be strengthened or they must be abandoned. In the former case, prejudices and habits of thought which up to that time have been lightly taken for granted, or only accepted half jokingly, must be more deeply accepted, must assume the force of dogma—of fixed, immovable truths—if they are to be strong enough to repel the invader. And once this has been done it can only with difficulty be undone. The next attack will have to be a far stronger one than before if it is to have any hope of making a breach. Real life examples of this are so common as to be over-familiar and therefore unnoticed. A good fictional example, however, is Henry Crawford in Jane Austen's *Mansfield Park*. His gay selfishness has protected him against any impulse to generosity that might have upset his comfort. These impulses have not in fact been very strong but his resistance to them has established a habit of selfishness. His passion for Fanny, which begins with a mere flirtation motivated by vanity, grows stronger and stronger. In the end it bids fair to overcome all his selfishness and develop the good qualities which are clearly there. He could be, we can see, not only a charming but a warm, sensitive and generous-hearted man. But his habits of self-indulgence are too strong. Entangled by his own vanity he elopes with Maria, whom he despises. Henry's further career is left to our imagination, with the suggestion that it will contain 'no small portion of vexation and regret'. There is no hint that he would ever be likely to love again as he had loved Fanny—and this is in keeping with ordinary observation. The defences of vanity and selfishness were too strong for his passion for Fanny to break through them completely. Afterwards they will be stronger still, because the alternative is intolerable remorse and humiliation. 'Vexation' is Jane Austen's prophecy for her villain, and vexation is a self-justifying anger, not the sorrow of repentance that leads to the possibility of new love.

There are many, many people who have successfully resisted the attacks of enthusiasm or passion by such means. There are many more who have not had to strengthen the defences suddenly or greatly but have gradually built up a sufficient defence by small degrees in response to almost unnoticed minor threats to personal comfort and peace of mind. The supreme example of this is Mr Woodhouse, in *Emma*, whose gentle self-indulgence and pre-occupation with his health plays on the affection of others so as to make sure that he shall always be surrounded by the care and comfort that he regards as his due. His tyranny is softened and disguised by his (equally self-centred) attention to the comfort of others.

Such well-defended personalities form the majority of the human race, and at this stage of its evolution that is just as well. But the fact remains that such a system of defences does preserve one kind of maturity, that of a balance of opposed tendencies (one set conscious, one unconscious), at the expense of the possibility of achieving the other kind of maturity which lies in a greater and deeper self-knowledge, a release of powers within the person. This can only come about by the abandonment of the defences, with all the danger and suffering that that involves.

The chief danger, the one which gives such force to the arguments of those who distrust passion, is that passion may attach itself to a symbol that can only lead to misery and destruction. Passion requires a symbol, since its striving is towards a reality which cannot be grasped in itself. The unconscious reality can only be grasped by means of a symbol, which relates more to the needs of the subject than to the nature of the object. Emma Bovary is the classic example of a woman casting herself into passionate relationships with men who do not correspond in any way to the imaginative image which she has formed of them. Their real nature could not possibly create the relationship for which she longs. The disaster may not be in all cases so complete but it requires very great generosity and courage to avoid bitterness. The wretched heroine of *Washington Square* could not achieve this generosity, but some have. Even the tragedy of misplaced passion can liberate, and the Marschallin in *Der Rosenkavalier* shows this process of painful maturing very well.

It is reasonable to consider that such a price is too high, that society could well do without people who have achieved this kind of maturity. It is not reasonable to deny that the price has to be paid, or that there is also a price paid for the preservation of the defences, in loss of sensibility and in lessened ability to love. It is a choice that only a certain number have to make in its clearest form. For most it never appears as a choice at all. But when the clear choice does occur it cannot be avoided, although it is of course possible to persuade oneself afterwards that the possibility of abandoning the defences and facing the deeper personal reality was really an illusion, that there was in fact no choice.

A clear choice of this kind is described in a very bad book by R. H. Benson, called *A Winnowing*, in which a nice, rich, cricket-playing young husband is restored to life from apparent death at the prayer of his wife, and reveals to her that his experience has unveiled to him the 'inwardness' of life to such a degree that the only proper response is the abandonment of all the normal pleasures and pastimes of his class so as to free him for work for other people, for prayer and study and the pursuit of perfection. But the first impact of the experience fades, he is drawn back gradually into the acceptance of all that he had decided to reject as irrelevant to his vision. And as he does so he justifies his withdrawal, persuading himself that it was all a silly dream, a sick man's enthusiasm, an escape from the stark realities of cucumber sandwiches and one's duty to the county.

As the extended researches of Jung, as well as more casual observations, seem to show, this crucial choice is one which is liable to present itself in a particularly clear-cut form when the passing of early youth has allowed time for a fairly well-developed adjustment to living. But the choice then made is likely to depend to some extent on the response to similar but less obviously crucial challenges encountered in earlier years. But we must still ask whether the deep and radical choices presented at certain stages of development are an invitation to a further stage of the search for the real self or merely a threat to the only kind of perfection which it is reasonable for the human animal to desire, that state of truce with the irrational in man which is the personal equivalent of civilisation.

It is perhaps relevant to notice that those who regard passion as an emotional excrescence, a parasite on the simple truth of 'pure' sex, are at pains to explain this to themselves and to other people. Those who accept the demands that passion makes upon them feel no need to justify themselves. They are responding to something that appears to them to be absolutely authentic, an impulse springing from their deepest self. If, later on, they reject the relationship involved they will then deny the reality of the experience. There is, then, at least a case for regarding the experience of sexual passion, of real 'falling in love', as of crucial significance in human development.

It is not only those who are still in the grip of passion who are found to defend it. Its best defenders are those who, in their time, responded to it and allowed it to form their lives. They have lived out its implications and their lives have justified them. Such people may never attempt, or see the need for, an intellectual justification of passion, but they know its significance as a matter of experience. They are often regarded as sentimental by the denouncers of passion because they look with indulgence and even approval on the young in the grip of this bewildering emotion. But sentimentality is emotion artificially attached to an object to which it is not essentially linked. Therefore those who deny the human authenticity of passion are bound to regard its upholders as sentimental. The sad thing about this labelling of passion is that the power of young love to arouse sympathetic emotion can easily be exploited so that this emotion *becomes* sentimental—that is, a response artificially created in people whose authentic response to passion is non-existent. This makes them feel that they are people of sensibility when they are only people of sentimentality, and it has the further, disastrous, effect of placing a thick layer of inauthentic sentiment around the experience of passion, one which makes it very difficult to distinguish the real thing from the mass-produced sham. This is true to such an extent that even those who respond to an authentic passion learn to do so within the convention of sentiment about romantic love, so that a perfectly real emotion can express itself in phrases and actions redolent of fourth-rate fiction.

What, then, are the effects of real passion which enable us to distinguish it from its synthetic substitutes? The essential difference is that passion is outward-looking, concentrated upon its object, whereas romantic sentiment cares only about the feeling produced. But this is an interior difference. The external test is one that can be observed. The first thing to notice is that passion alters people's behaviour, sometimes to such an extent that they seem scarcely recognisable, even to themselves. Unless we are to assume, as the ancients did, that this is an enchantment inflicted by the gods (and maybe they were not so far wrong) we must suppose that the change in behaviour is due to the release of certain elements in the personality which have not previously been able to express their existence outwardly. The impulse of passion is impatient of convention, of custom, of anything inward or outward which prevents the attainment of its object. It is easy to regard this object as simply physical union with the beloved, but, if that were all, why does the emotion continue unabated and even more violently during the course of a—sometimes long—love affair? And why, if physical union is the sole object, does it have to be union with one particular person, to a point at which even a very highly-sexed person becomes totally indifferent to the charms of others who may be much better endowed—physically, emotionally and intellectually—than the beloved? The answer is that real passion is part of the search for the authentic self. At a certain point, the personality which has relied on 'the Law'—custom and accepted ideas about itself and its environment—is no longer content with these as a definition of self, and needs to discover itself at a deeper level. This need is expressed, typically, in the restlessness and discontent which characterise adolescence. Like all human phenomena which appear to be sudden and unexpected, falling in love is really the break-through to the conscious level of processes which have been going on under the surface for a long time, the overt symptoms of which have probably been observable but generally not properly interpreted. This is noticeable also in the case of 'conversion', religious or otherwise, which appears to be sudden and 'out of the blue' but which closer examination of the history of the person concerned reveals as the culmination of a long process, as in the case of St Augustine, or of Pascal.

I am, in fact, suggesting that falling in love has the same psychological significance as such a 'conversion'. What it does is to release the individual from some of the layers of 'the flesh', it sets free for him the world of 'the spirit'. The spirit, in so far as it has thus become accessible or usable, finds it possible to ignore the demands of the flesh. The degree to which it can do so is determined by the strength of established habits of thought, and the strength of the interior force that has been released. The strength of this impulse is the strength of the need for self knowledge, not mere theoretical knowledge about oneself but the knowledge which is direct access to and experience of areas of oneself which were formerly unguessed at. The fact that this impulse is so strong is an indication that it serves some purpose which is essential to human life, and that its suppression or denigration is not a denial of a superficial annoyance but the closing of the gateway to the fullness of being human. In that case we can only deny or ignore its implications at the cost of denying the validity of man's age-long aspiration towards wholeness and freedom.

But if the impulse of passion is essentially towards the liberation of the self—the spirit—from the flesh why is it normally directed towards another human being?

Knowledge (the 'light' of St John's gospel) is not private, it is of its nature to be shared. We can only know ourselves by knowing each other, the way of self-knowledge is the way of love, there is no other. To direct this impulse towards wholeness there must be something to give conscious direction to it, an immediate and conscious object, for in itself the need for self knowledge—the drive towards wholeness—is not experienced consciously. In order to bring about the conditions for the wholeness it craves the human self must have in the conscious mind some symbol towards which its energies can be directed. This symbol is generally another human being, and that human being one who is sexually desired, but the sexual attraction is only the trigger that releases the forces that are driving towards wholeness. This human being immediately acquires attributes which have little or nothing to do with his own 'real' self, as it is observed by other people who are not in love. The beloved is the object of a desire which is insatiable, the desire for human perfection, and he or she must act as symbol for this reality which cannot be directly apprehended.

Does this mean that the impulse of passion is in fact self-directed, 'selfish' in the ordinary sense? It depends on what one means by 'self'. If the self is an essentially isolated thing whose best hope of happiness lies in that isolation, then passion is selfish in the ordinary sense, and the beloved merely a symbol for part of the private self which can be discovered in no other way. But if the self is in fact the 'point' in the human person at which he is in contact with other persons (the 'spirit' of Pauline psychology) then passion is the means of establishing a real communication 'in the spirit'. Self-knowledge, then, has two senses which are really one, for the opening up of the deeper layers of personality gives access to that self in which alone a real meeting is possible.

In this connection a passage from Anthony Storr's book *The Integrity of Personality* is relevant:

'I believe it can generally be shown that these people [the objects of a childish or adolescent 'crush' or 'passion'] epitomise undeveloped parts of the child's own personality, and that they attract him so strongly because they stir a subjective response. It seems probable that those parts of the personality which are latent, undeveloped and only potential—those parts, therefore, which can be said to be *unconscious*—are in fact recognised by the person concerned, but, to start with, are thought to belong to others rather than to himself. The child can be said, as it were, to "fall in love" with his own latent potentialities.'

And later on in the book the theme is taken up again:

'The Greeks of the fifth century B.C. [quoted in an excerpt from the Symposium] evidently felt the same need as ourselves for an explanation of the compulsive and magical quality of love, and recognised the subjective element which they personi-fied as the lost half of a bisected whole. In finding a lover a man was therefore discovering the other side of himself, and the same was true for a woman . . . The high value which the Greeks attributed to masculinity, and the comparatively lowly position of woman in their society, perhaps explains why male homo-sexual love was valued above the love of woman . . . But we can entirely agree with the conception of the desire and pursuit of the whole, and with the idea that people in love are seeking not only for sexual satisfaction but for the other half of themselves.'

But if passion is the opening up of the personality, a step towards full self-knowledge, what is the significance of the fact that passion is normally sexual passion? There are many other forms of passion. The symbol which focuses the efforts of the spirit in its struggle to break free of the flesh can be a political or social cause, God, a pop star or an art or vocation, or sometimes much less apparently 'good' things, such as wealth or personal power. It can be something as grandiose as the desire to convert mankind to a new religion, or as humble as a little bit of garden to cultivate. If all these things, apparently so varied in type and value, can be the effective symbols of personal wholeness, is there any reason to suppose that passion is essentially connected with sex? Are the other things substitutes for sex, and if so why, and to what extent are they satisfactory ones?

In order to answer these questions it is necessary to see how passion (any kind of passion) actually works. First of all there is the real, perceptible and indeed obvious break-through of a hidden force. This force, which is needed to make the break in the protective (and necessary) layers of custom and habitual ways of thought and behaviour, carries the whole person forward under its own impetus for some time. But not for ever. The impulse slackens. The tendency of the flesh, when this happens, is to cover over the breach thus made and return to 'normal'. This can only be prevented if the person is sufficiently aware of the value of what has been gained by this breakthrough to try, consciously and deliberately, to keep the channel of communication open and even enlarge it. The kinds of behaviour which were easy under the original impetus of passion must be continued without its help. This effort has to be sustained over a long period or the channel will soon fill up again, and in order to do this the effort must continue to 'make sense' even when the emotion had faded. It must, in fact, make *sense* and not just feeling, if it is to endure. The symbol (from garden plot to universal salvation) which focused the emotion must continue to make sense, and this sense, or meaning, must be expressed in action that bears some relation to it. The symbol must be made to reveal the reality it indicates by being made to '*work*' in a way which is satisfactory both to the emotions and the mind. This is precisely what sexual intercourse does in a relationship, if the mutual passion is one between people whose temperament and circumstances make a permanent relationship a real possibility.

When people fall in love their physical desire for each other is a desire to express the impulse towards knowledge of the self by means of an action that aims at destroying as far as possible all barriers between them. The complete mutual giving of loving sexual intercourse is both an expression of the desire to break free of the 'enclosure' of the flesh and the obvious means of bringing about this liberation. It is the means of changing the symbol of liberation (the 'object' of passion) into the reality which is the effective freedom of action of 'the spirit'. It involves, potentially at least, the whole person, and this whole self-giving is the ideal of lovers, though temperament and various kinds of educational and cultural conditioning must make this finally impossible. But even if the exchange is not as perfect in practice as in desire, the sexual expression of passion may be regarded as the norm or 'type' of all passion because it contains within itself, by nature, the conditions for its own development towards wholeness, and needs no help from outside. It is not a question of choosing the best form in which to express sexual passion; the desire for this expression is built into the nature of the sexual emotion itself. Sexual intercourse is action that brings into play the powers newly discovered, directing them 'outwards' in the sense that they are put at the service not only of the personal self but of the other self in whom is the symbol of self-discovery. It is a matter of experience that lovers who are afraid of missing their own physical satisfaction and therefore concentrate their attention on themselves do not in fact achieve the highest degree even of purely physical satisfaction, because this is found only in a very subtle mutuality. This is only rarely achieved with ease. More often it is the result of effort and 'unselfishness' which cares more (or at least takes more trouble over) the other person than over its own satisfaction. This is the way in which sex, of its very nature, directs the impulse of passion into the way in which it has the best chance to bring about a real and permanent change within the person. On the other hand it is not at all difficult to prevent it from doing anything of the kind. So ingenious and resourceful is the flesh in protecting itself from the attacks of the spirit that it can even render harmless to itself the achievement of a high degree of sexual mutuality, which comes about normally by the exercise of the care and self-giving impulse of love. It is, in fact, nonsense for the advocates of love in sex-relations to claim that the highest kind of physical satisfaction can only be achieved by those who sincerely love each other, unless one uses the word 'highest' in a sense which takes it right out of the sphere of purely physical experience and therefore makes it inappropriate. It is possible to achieve a high degree of sexual pleasure (or more accurately sexual happiness, because it is a very real though limited happiness) and yet frustrate the tendency of this happiness to spread into the whole of living. There are degrees of this separation, and it is unlikely that both partners will do it in the same way. One of them may keep his or her sexual experience separate only because the other demands it and that is the price that must be paid for having it at all, but as long as the separation exists the spirit is being prevented to some extent from using sex as its way of overcoming the flesh.

This is not intended as an accusation. The achievement of a modus vivendi in the flesh is no small one, and it may sometimes be the only alternative to personal disintegration. Nor does such a 'civilisation' of the conscious and unconscious areas of personality into a reasonable working unit mean that the spirit is doomed to remain forever imprisoned. As far as sex is concerned, the refusal to translate the impulse of passion into a whole personal action in accordance with its natural tendency means that, inevitably, 'a great prince in prison lies'. But passion can take other than sexual forms, and may be far more effective by doing so. The cult of 'normality' has its drawbacks. But the thing that makes it clear that sexual passion is 'normal' as well as common is that its ability to provide the means for self-knowledge and the pursuit of wholeness is part of its natural 'shape'.

So in practice a 'substitute' may produce greater human achievement and a more complete liberation of the self than sex can normally do. In this case it is a substitute only in the sense that its effect does not so obviously belong to it by nature. Any 'substitute' must be capable of providing the same psychological conditions as sexual passion. It must provide both a symbol to focus the impulse of passion, and an activity which is related to the symbol and serves to embody the relationship in concrete, practical terms. The success of the substitution will depend on the suitability of the chosen activity to provide, in practice, the sort of concrete, personally satisfying achievement that will be equivalent to the feeling of completeness and emotional contentment that can result from a really satisfactory sexual relationship. This is why it is not merely an *a priori* moral judgment to say that such things as the pursuit of wealth, power (including spiritual power), sensation, and so on, are 'fake' or 'bad' or a waste of talents. They are fake, bad, wasteful of human potentialities because, as a matter of experience, their achievement does not provide the sense of wholeness and contentment that their use as a symbol seemed to promise.

Passion demands to be translated into effective outward action, and if it is prevented from doing so it turns sour and corrupts, producing the kind of behaviour we label 'decadent'. Decadence is not the result of the freeing of passion from restrictions, it is rather the result of the frustration of its proper development. Denied its natural, essentially constructive, outlets it turns on itself and squanders its energy in self-destructive activity which blinds rather than enlightens. What it lacks is the element of relationship, which is so clearly present in sexual passion and whose necessity for all true development I discussed in the last chapter.

Passion, therefore—of which sexual passion is, as St Paul indicates, the obvious 'type'—is an impulse towards human wholeness and freedom, but one which requires a compelling imaginative symbol to focus its energy, and the possibility of some personal devotion equivalent to the self-giving gesture of sexual intercourse.

This is also the ideal which is presented with inescapable clarity and force in the gospels. The 'passionate' quality of this ideal is shown by the fact that the 'Establishment' of the period regarded Christ as a man who led the people astray and threatened the stability of Church and State. This is the immemorial attitude of any Establishment to passion or enthusiasm in all its forms, and it has also characterised the later attitude of the Christian Church when, in its time, it became a political organism.

The situation in this latter case was complicated by the fact that the Church's 'raison d'être' was the transmission of a message which was psychological dynamite, with the result that organisation of Christianity as a religion has been in a state of unacknowledged internal tension throughout its history, a tension which has given the characteristic shape to the phases of its development. The tension is, in fact, not only necessary but beneficial and is the only means so far discovered of making Christianity safe to handle. The fact that nowadays it seems as if the old safety precautions may end up by guarding an empty tomb does not invalidate the historical function of the Church. (But the historical justification does not justify some of the forms which the organism has taken or the methods by which it exercised its necessary function.)

The chief note of Christ's summons is one of ruthlessness, of disregard for convention or, apparently, for the common decencies and obligations of normal living. 'Let the dead bury their dead', he told a man who wanted to wait until his aged father had died before he joined the followers of the Christ, 'but as for you, go and proclaim the Kingdom of God'.

'No one who puts his hand to the plough and looks back is fit for the Kingdom of God.'

'He who loves father or mother more than me is not worthy of me.'

Examples could be multiplied, for this absolute demand echoes throughout all four gospels, but this last quotation brings to mind the description of the demands of a sexual relationship given in Genesis, when the man was given a mate of his own kind 'because it is not good for man to be alone' (a phrase which demonstrates how deep and permanent in the mind of man is the conviction that human beings can only live completely in relationship) and the passage concludes: 'For this cause a man will leave his mother and father and be joined to his wife, and they shall be two in one body.' Christ's comment on this passage is 'Therefore what God has joined together it is not for man to part.'

The gospel demand for total dedication is the one that passion makes in its various forms. The demand of the self to be allowed to discover and complete itself is so strong that none of the good and necessary ties of affection or loyalty can be allowed to stand in the way. And the 'two in one body' of sexual love, or what Donne called a 'dialogue of one', is only the typical expression of the necessary condition for the fulfilment of this demand—that of a real, not merely a formal, relationship, worked out in practical action of a kind that has an essential relation to the nature of the demand. And in considering Christ's comment—on which the age-long Christian insistence on marital fidelity has rested—the psychological truth of his words becomes clear if we replace the terms of his own characteristic antithesis with those which St Paul generally uses when he wants to make the same contrast: 'What the spirit has joined together it is not for the flesh to part.'

The demands of the flesh are legitimate and necessary, by it and with it man has managed to exist and develop through the centuries. But when the spirit makes its demands they are paramount. This order of importance is typified by Christ's own formula of authority: 'It was said to the men of old . . . but *I* say to you . . .', he who is the spokesman of the spirit. These demands are concerned not with what man is, in the flesh, but with what he can be, even now, and can become. But he has to start somewhere, and that 'where' is the point at which passion makes its demand to 'sell all that thou hast, and come, follow me'. The Commandments of the Law which the rich young man in the gospel story had 'kept from his youth', are necessary and good, they are the prerequisite without which the conscience of man is too muddled and distorted to be able to distinguish the authentic demand of passion from the fantasies of escapism and self-indulgence. But they are not enough, in themselves, to satisfy the need of the spirit for self-discovery. From the moral security of obedience to the Law the spirit must go out in response to the call which is that of a man's own deepest nature, and which is expressed in the gospel in all its uncompromising clarity:

'No man can serve two masters.'

'Repent (be transformed) for the Kingdom of Heaven is here.'

'He who would save his life will lose it, but whoever loses his life for my sake—he will save it.'

But when the call has been heard, and the initial response made, the other essential condition of the fulfilment of the meaning of passion makes it demand. 'By this all men will know that you are my disciples, if you have love for one another.' And he made it clear on many occasions that this love was expressed essentially in direct, personal service, the relief of want, the bringing of healing and hope, comfort and forgiveness. This service must not rely on any form of emotional exaltation but must continue over a long, long period when the symbol that passion finds has no longer the power to evoke any emotion, but has become merely the coat-of-arms of a prince who has been absent so long that his very existence is in doubt. But because the 'joining together' in the spirit brought about in response to passion is a fact operating at the deepest level of personality it can only be 'parted' at the cost of undoing all that has been achieved, and denying (as so many do) the reality or relevance of anything but the legitimate and reasonable demands of the flesh.

This saying of Christ is, it seems, true in the clearest possible way. It is not equally clear, however, that it can be applied in any simple or fool-proof way to the question of divorce, and although the discussion of this thorny question is outside the scope of this book it is perhaps worth noting that if we are to insist that 'what God has joined it is not for man to part' we have to be very sure that we know what are the conditions on which 'God joins', and perhaps cautious of equating it with what the Church or the State has joined. We should also be less ready to assume that authentic response to the demands of the spirit is best assisted by demanding from people who have barely begun to emerge from the nursery of the flesh the kind of behaviour which is proper to a person in whom the spirit has achieved a near-complete victory. The result of demanding heroism from people who are not ready for it is generally not true heroism but either an exalted kind of hypocrisy or discouragement and despair. And the means traditionally used in the attempt to enforce heroic standards on people for whom they are in no way real are, commonly, a well-developed technique of emotional blackmail combined with fake logic and pious bribery. There is a good, fictional, example of this in a well-known novel called *The Cardinal*, in a scene in which the young priest-hero persuades his sister to give up the young Jew she loves, for the sake of her family. He plays on her love of her parents, and she consents. The disastrous results are unfolded throughout a large part of the book. This is no new situation. 'They (the guardians of religion) bind heavy burdens, hard to bear, and lay them on men's shoulders, but they themselves will not move them with their finger. They do all their deeds to be seen by men... they love the place of honour . . . and being called "Teacher" by men. But you are not to be called "Teacher", for you have one teacher and you are all brothers.'

This teacher is the spirit which is Christ's own and which makes itself felt in those who are 'of God'. It speaks in the depth of the heart, it is the 'spirit of the truth' who will 'lead you into all truth'. The ways in which this truth is discovered are ways of the flesh—they must be—but they must serve the spirit in humility. The great enemy of the spirit is hypocrisy. It is a real danger to people with high ideals, because it can become a personal protection from the demands of the spirit, by substituting for them others which belong only to the Law. It also serves as a means of reassuring oneself of one's worthiness and 'rightness' when it can be imposed on other people, whose conformity provides the evidence required for such reassurance. But, as Christ made clear, this is clean contrary to the real nature of the Kingdom of Heaven. 'Woe to you, Scribes and Pharisees, hypocrites! for you are like white-washed tombs, which outwardly appear beautiful, but within they are full of dead men's bones, and all uncleanness.'

'Dead men's bones' is as perfect an image as one could desire of what might be called sentimental morality. This is the attempt to attach the emotions proper to the authentic impulse of passion to the forms (the Law) which in fact can be no more than a support to the impulse of passion. But sentimental morality uses these forms not as a support for spirit but as a substitute for it. Thus in the incident in *The Cardinal*, family loyalty was used not to support the desire of the girl to grow up but as a substitute for personal decision. A plain statement that 'your love is against the moral law' might have been harsh or untrue, but not hypocritical. For the hypocrisy of sentimental morality is worse than pure legalism, which is—if sometimes unjust—strong and safe and rational, and leaves the spirit free to discover itself. Hypocrisy imposes sentimental or 'fake' morality as a duty, and it is hard indeed for these bones to 'hear the voice of the Lord', and be clothed in the flesh of authentic passion.

Hypocrisy was the one thing that Christ would not tolerate, because it is the one thing which destroys utterly the ability to hear and respond to the call of passion to 'leave all things'. There are many things which can prevent a man from achieving wholeness, but hypocrisy prevents him from even trying because it persuades him that he has it. It fobs him off with a sham and so kills his desire for the real. This is the 'blasphemy against the holy spirit' which Christ described as the unforgiveable sin.

CHAPTER V

'THE BREAD WHICH WE SHARE'

The individual in the community

THE first impulse of the spirit seeking freedom is typified by sexual passion and this is why I have used the word 'passion' to describe the thrust towards self-discovery as the spirit, the real self, struggles for freedom. It is something which, as we have seen, can only be realised in a relationship, however much private thought, reflection, study may assist the realisation. But the typical relationship, the sexual one, does not exist and cannot develop in isolation. It is set in a community. The couple draw out of the community to find each other, but they must also return to it.

Does this placing of a sexual (or other close functional) relationship in a community setting represent merely a necessary accommodation to circumstances, or is it essential to the relationship itself? To put it another way, does the natural development of the relationship demand a social setting for its fulfilment? If so, what does this imply about the nature of social relationships at the service of self-discovery?

What is the link (if there is one) between private personal relationships, and public or communal ones? The Christian notion is that there should be no opposition between the two, but rather that each should assist the other; yet in the world as we know it the two are constantly in conflict. This conflict provides material for a never-ending succession of novels, plays, treatises and poems, it provokes moral theology, civics, and sociology. And it is this conflict that creates the crises of conscience that so frequently and tragically face those who try to respond to the inexorable demands of passion. If the Christian claim to serve the perfection of human living means anything it must show a recognition of this problem and some indication of the sort of means by which the conflict may be resolved.

Those who revolt against the hypocrisy of the mass, against the formality of institutions with their sentimental morality, are driven to look for a philosophy which seeks truth in the individual's separated search for personal integrity. The individual must tear himself away from the support of the Law, they feel, if he is to discover his eternal self and come face to face with God in the wilderness. Kierkegaard and Simone Weil saw this as the only possible choice for a Christian who would not compromise his faith, and Nietzsche rejected Christianity because it seemed inextricably involved in the life of the heavy mass who are content to take orders and have no desire for freedom. Even those who have stressed the necessity of community for human living have seen it as a ballast for the spirit, a framework to control and contain the individual striving for self-knowledge.

The human community does serve this purpose and, distressing as it may be to the individual consumed by the conviction that his humanity requires a passionate pursuit of freedom, it is in fact seldom possible to achieve even a proximate freedom in isolation. The disintegrating effect of solitude on all but those who have already achieved maturity has been proved by experiment, reported from experience such as that of prisoners under the Nazis, and reconstructed in fiction from *The Count of Monte Cristo* to *The Prisoner*.

The organisation of community living is the expression of the fact that we do live in the flesh, whether we like it or not, and must take it into account. The inner response of passion, the Kierkegaardian 'aesthetic' reaction of immediate and personal commitment, remains unfulfilled without its expression in action which is at least implicitly relational.

The passionate or 'aesthetic' response that refuses to translate its initial emotional experience into action can only try to rediscover itself in repeating the experience with increasing disillusion and despair. What Kierkegaard calls the ethical level is in fact the working out of passion, according to its intrinsic nature as it is typified in a sexual relationship. And his religious level is concerned with the need for a directing symbol which is, as I suggested in the last chapter, the function of the beloved in sexual passion.

The religious symbol focuses the Christian (or other religious) commitment to search, and the pattern of this commitment is, as I have tried to show, identical with the pattern which is inherent in the development of the normal sexual relationship.

The religious commitment is not necessarily a communal one, but Christianity is essentially a communal religion. This is not simply a utilitarian adaptation of the basic individual commitment but is due to Christ's recognition that the individual in isolation is forever incomplete. This is shown by a further examination of the natural development of a sexual relationship (to which St Paul compared the internal relationship within the people of God) as it enters its second stage.

The first stage begins under the impulse of passion and is characterised by the psychological isolation of the couple. This isolation occurs even when the passion is one-sided, or when it takes a non-sexual form. Other people, other interests, become unimportant, so many bits of furniture, the necessary but irrelevant setting for the pursuit of the one absorbing symbol. The individual's entire personality is concentrated on the effort to discover, to 'know' the object of passion as completely as possible, indeed to a degree which is not at all possible. This isolation and concentration necessarily alters the ordinary sense of values to a greater or lesser extent, it ignores or rejects ordinary behaviour and ordinary loyalties if these appear to interfere with it. This need for rejection, as I showed in the last chapter, is brutally clear in many passages of the gospels, and so it is natural for the passionate Christian to suppose that accommodation to normal values can only be a compromise with the flesh and a flight from the demands of the spirit. It is equally natural that those who can see Christianity only in terms of its organisation—that is, as of necessity a community 'in the flesh'—should reject it violently and absolutely. But the study of the natural development of a sexual relationship shows that this is a misreading both ways. The isolation is a stage, and its purpose is to establish a community of love in which the person, summoned to self-discovery by passion, may dedicate himself to the service of that which is symbolised by the object of passion. He becomes detached from all that might interfere with his dedication, even, apparently, from the 'home'—whether actual family or nationality, ideology, creed or other community with its codes and values—that bred him and formed him. But only for a time. The 'new community' created by passion becomes in this way established and strong, the doorway made for the spirit can be fixed permanently open, and through it, quite naturally, the communication of the spirit extends itself. Its first extension is to the knowledge and service of the beloved as one who may be understood and appreciated, studied and served. He or she ceases to be purely a symbol (which is essentially un-intellectual and even unconscious in its working) but becomes another 'person' having an existence outside the scope of his function as symbol. This is the beginning of love.

As Erich Fromm[1] says:

> 'The basic affirmation contained in love is directed towards the beloved person as an incarnation of essentially human qualities [this is equivalent to 'the spirit' of Pauline psychology]. Love for one person implies love for man [i.e. man's real self, the spirit] as such. Love for man as such is not, as it is frequently supposed to be, an abstraction coming 'after' the love for a specific person, or an enlargement of the experience with a specific 'object'; it is its premise, although, genetically, it is acquired in contact with concrete individuals.'

Once this has happened, it is possible for the kind of personal devotion discovered and made possible by the commitment of passion to be extended to others with whom the relationship is not initiated by passion as such. But because of the change which passion has brought about it has the chance to be a different kind of relationship from that inculcated simply by the way custom—ethical or social—modifies inclination, and its roots will be in the new view of life and love acquired under the influence of passion. It may, and will, express itself in exactly the same kind of actions

[1] Erich Fromm, *The Fear of Freedom*, Routledge and Kegan Paul, London, 1952, p. 99.

as are encouraged by a well-developed and humane moral and ethical code (St Paul's 'Law'), but it has a different character. What makes it work is not the necessary conditioning of an education in good moral habits (in the flesh) but the authentic impulse of the spirit.

This change is such a normal thing, so much a matter of everyday observation, that we take it for granted. It is typified and normally brought about in that natural result of a sexual relationship which is the conception and birth of a child. The community of love that has been formed between the parents is extended to form a relationship with the children which possesses the same character of authenticity as that initiated between the parents by mutual passion. Sometimes, indeed, the emotion of maternal or paternal love is the first experience of real 'passion'. This happens, for instance, when the couple's married relationship has not been truly 'passionate'. It may be that one or other was seeking a dependent child-parent relationship in marriage. This happens when the dependent stage has not been outgrown in the normal way and a 'grown-up' relationship is therefore not yet possible.

There is no necessary dividing line at all between behaviour that springs from this authentic love and behaviour that is according to morality, custom and inclination. We do not transcend the flesh all in a moment, and the authentic impulse of the spirit is not strong enough or consistent enough to be the sole motive of behaviour, at least at this stage. It is, it must be, 'blind' because its sole means of action is still in the flesh, which is enclosed by ignorance. The relations between parents and children, and also between lovers, depend on the continuing framework of custom and morality to support them. Moral codes, ethical systems, the phenomenon known as civilisation, may not be authentic in the sense that they spring directly from the demands of the real self, the spirit, but they are necessary. There can be no true freedom without the Law as its guarantor. Behaviour according to the Law, which is essentially concerned with the flesh, reacts on and is acted on by authentic behaviour according to the spirit, and the aim of a humane society must be to make it possible for the spirit to achieve freedom by shaping its customs more and more closely to the needs of the spirit.

This is a fact, but for that very reason it is apt to make people think that such 'shaping' is all that is required, and that the community and the values governing it can only serve individual self-discovery by approximating as closely as may be to its needs, or at least by trying not to put more difficulties in the way than are demanded by the necessities of justice and public order.

The Christian notion of the function of the community is, however, ultimately a spiritual one, but this does not mean that it contradicts the legitimate demands of the flesh.

The aspect of life in the flesh with which we are concerned here is the life in the community, not that of the individual, and it is therefore better described by that familiar phrase 'the world', which has no connection with 'worldliness' or 'materialism' in the pejorative sense but simply refers to the fact of human community-life which, since it is lived by people 'in the flesh', must accommodate itself to this state. It is in this sense that St John's gospel, whose vision of human potentialities opens up the idea of a community in the spirit, speaks of the followers of Christ being 'in the world' in a way in which he himself was not, and can yet say that they are not 'of the world'. But St John emphasises that they are not to be taken 'out of the world'. Their work is in the world, Christ himself is sending them into the world, to be inextricably in it and for it. The command to 'give to Caesar what is Caesar's and to God what is God's', is not simply a recommendation to keep the sacred and the secular each to their own spheres. It is rather a recognition of the fact that the world and the spirit must both be considered, but that to confuse them is of benefit to neither. To reduce the impulse towards freedom to an attempt to establish better and better social and political systems is to confuse the two; but to despise or ignore the structure of public morality and responsibility in favour of esoteric and exclusive soul-cultivation is to cripple the spirit rather than to free it.

Faced with this conflict we can perceive it as a complete impasse, which we must accept and put up with. Or we can evade the

issue by ignoring the community as far as possible and concentrating on the needs of the exceptional—the genius, the super-man.
Or we can put the community first, proclaiming that this will
supply the 'real' needs of the individual also. None of these
'solutions' is satisfactory, though we can persuade ourselves into
supposing that one of them is, if not satisfactory, at least acceptable
in practice. It is perhaps more honest to admit that the problem is
insoluble, at least as long as it is presented in the terms in which
we are accustomed to consider it.

But it is one of the distinguishing marks of the gospel idea of the
meaning of being human that it refuses to subordinate either the
individual to the community or the community to the individual,
and the stalemate which seems therefore inevitable turns out to be
a conceptual, not an actual one.

This is not as Utopian as it appears when we consider the very
ordinary fact of life in a normally happy family. External standards
and rules are applied in a family because they are needed in any
community 'in the world' consisting of people who are still 'in
the flesh'. But it is a matter of everyday fact that a family does
not operate *by* these rules and standards, it only *uses* them. A
family that lives by rules is rightly regarded as peculiar, unloving
and 'inhuman'—a very revealing adjective. The rules are there to
protect and support the development of each individual, but this
development takes place not just *in* the family community but *by*
the community. Each one takes and gives, from and to each other
one, what he or she needs and can give. Morality as a code, and
religion or ideology as a symbol, are there to act as checks and
guides to the developing relationships which, among the children
at least, are only potentially 'spiritual'. The aim of all this is to
form behaviour in the flesh so that the person will not be too
resistant to the impulse of the spirit when a stage is reached at
which reactions and ideas, however good, which have been acquired from the parents must be transcended in the drive towards
the freedom of personal wholeness. So it comes about that behaviour
that is authentic in the parents, springing from their own response
to the demands of the spirit, can create relationships with and

between the children which are at least germinally of the spirit in kind, but which make use of the Law not to imprison but to create the conditions for freedom.

This is what the Law, which Christ said he intended not to destroy but to fulfil, should do. In this way the isolation into which passion draws those who respond to it does not really cut people off from the community. It only withdraws them from its 'fleshly' influences for a while in order that they may discover in themselves the power to create relationships which are authentic, of the spirit. This happens naturally and commonly to and through the children of a marriage. The children are those who naturally 'catch' the new capacity for loving which has been learnt in the extension of passion, and it spreads outwards from them and by them. This is so basic a part of the Christian understanding of life that in the apostolic period children born to Christian parents were not baptised, either in infancy or later. Their life in a Christian family was expected to be of such a nature as in itself to provide that opportunity for the breakthrough of the spirit which the baptismal ritual symbolises.

But however far it extends, however many and wide the relationships it includes, passion must, if it is not to degenerate, renew itself by contact with its source, by means of action related to the symbol which gave it birth. This is, as I suggested, the function of sex in a marriage, and it is also the function of religion or ideology in the community, from the family outwards.

It is becoming a truism of child psychology that if one stage of development is not properly appreciated and is therefore distorted, the next is also delayed or distorted and may even be prevented altogether. This is equally true of the development of a sexual relationship and of the overall personal development of which it is the centre and type. When passion appears as an end in itself and refuses to fulfil itself in action, thus extending naturally the scope of the 'new' self, it goes sour (for instance in the extremes of 'romantic' passion, as de Rougemont shows). But at the next stage also, when the 'light' which comes from response to the spirit is illuminating other relationships and both deepening and widening them, there is still no settling down. The symbol and act needed by passion continue to renew its meaning and power, but not forever in the same way. The symbol is not the reality, though it activates it, and as the action of the spirit increases and consolidates itself it needs less and less to rely on the power of the symbol and the acts that express a direct relation to it, because the reality is gradually becoming a matter of daily experience. This is why deeply devoted couples, as they get older, often do not require sex to recreate their relationship. The thing itself, the reality of the relationship in the spirit, has taken over so much of their life together and is so much something they simply know, that sex is no longer important in the same way. This is fairly rare, and has little to do with the cynical or merely tired indifference to sex. It is, in any case, perfectly baffling to the young who cannot imagine love except in terms of the act which expresses it. They are quite right. Sex, or its psychological equivalent, is necessary for survival; not only for the survival of the race through procreation but for the survival of the human in the race. Its meaning is enormous—but limited.

In the life of the community also this process of replacing the symbol by the reality appears to take place. The ideal state of affairs would be one in which the life both of the individual and of the community should be of the spirit, that is, authentic. The teaching of Christ is that this is possible, not just in some vague future state but at least germinally here and now.

The function of the response demanded of the man of faith, the response which I have described as that of passion, is to bring about in the individual that change of heart which later will naturally extend itself in a new capacity for authentic relationship. But if the process is to continue and grow and consolidate itself it must have both a characteristic symbol and a suitable means of giving the symbol expression in action, as the nature of passion demands. The symbol and action must be such as to bring into play different areas of personality—physical, emotional, intellectual —as the symbol and act of sexual love do. They must be capable of development so that the unimaginable reality which is symbolised and activated may gradually become a matter of experience. The aim must be that ultimately the very real necessity of the symbol as a symbol may be superseded by the untrammelled power of the thing itself. But since there are always people at different stages of personal development in the community the symbol cannot be outgrown in any absolute sense, though its significance will be different to people at different stages.

There is an ambiguity in Christian teaching which has obscured for many people, including many Christians, the nature of the central symbol which serves to focus the impulse towards wholeness, to provide it with action both effective and typical, and to indicate the way in which it may properly extend, renew and experience itself. This obscurity was the result of the tendency of Christians in the past to distinguish, separate and label in isolation aspects of life which clearly belong together. But this tendency is only an example of the normal need to analyse what was at first taken for granted. It is only in the light of the analysis that the real unity can be discovered and effectively used.

The Christian symbol, to be effective, must demonstrate its validity apart from the apparatus of proof, deduction and symbolism which have served to expound it. (Symbolism, in this context, is not the same as symbol. The symbol is an immediately apprehensible part of a whole which is not consciously apprehensible in its totality. Symbolism is the expression of a mysterious reality in terms of another, unrelated but intellectually parallel, reality, which is easily understood.) This intellectual clarification is essential, as it is essential for the art student to master the rules of perspective. Once these rules are thoroughly understood they become part of the way of seeing and feeling and are no longer necessary in themselves, except for the purpose of handing on knowledge. So the Christian symbol must be more than intellectually comprehensible. It must show itself to be the one which answers the needs and aspirations of man historically and perennially, in both his 'horizontal' and 'vertical' development. The needs and questions are old needs and questions, and the answers must be immediately and practically available now, as in the past.

It must be an answer which belongs to the nature of man as he experiences himself in the flesh, and as he half despairingly but obstinately wants to be in the spirit.

The conflict between daily life with its hopes and comforts and work and sorrows, and the unquenchable though apparently futile desire for liberation from this 'horizontal' existence is presented in its most intransigent form by the opposition between the needs of the individual and those of the community. If it is shown typically (in the strict sense of the word) in the conflict between the demands of passion and those of the 'home', we may expect the solution, if there is one, to be on the same lines as that imposed by the nature of a sexual relationship, with its characteristic stages and changes.

Human beings are always divided between the desire to secure the necessities and comforts of life in the flesh and the desire for 'something more', and the natural tendency is to safeguard the daily needs first. But every now and then someone is driven to say, 'Get your priorities right—do you really care most about things you know very well are essentially perishable? Something in yourself tells you that there is more to life than this, and this something is the voice of your real self. You know this, if you want to, because it says things that authenticate themselves, in relation to what you know of yourself, if only you will be honest.' But people labouring under the necessity of keeping on living, some- how or other, know very well that such 'knowledge', however authentic, has to be more than a subconscious reality. It must erupt into action, be visible, as true passion demands. It must express itself in 'work' that belongs to it—and the 'it' is a communal one. The answer to this need is that the work must spring from 'faith'—not merely the tentative openness of the honest mind (though this is the necessary beginning) but the full commitment of passion. In that case, a symbol or sign is required to focus the response of passion, and it is a fact of experience that human beings do demand such a sign. Their demand is, naturally, for something imaginable and concrete, for something that seems to combine the needs of flesh and spirit.

An example of this is the desire for a return to some communal 'golden age'. This is a symbol that the resulting human tendency to mythologise history can easily provide. But the authentic voice of the spirit, which is incurably realistic, has to keep on contradicting this very natural tendency. It says, in effect: the thing you want cannot be found in the past. The effort to re-create a perfect community from the mythical past is bound to remain work on the 'horizontal' plane, since the thing has never in fact existed but is only the symbol of something you want in the future. The new life you long for cannot come from the past, or from outside, it can only come from the deepest reality of yourselves, which is the spirit, dynamic love. And you can only discover this love, and the fact that it is love, by sharing it with 'the world' and so spreading this life whose very nature is to be shared. Thus the sharing of love will not *take the place of* the ordinary daily work which is necessary to human life, rather it will give it a *different human content*, as passion gives a new meaning to actions identical with those of the flesh.

It sounds so simple that it is tempting to say: in that case all we have to do is teach people to be more loving, and the question reduces itself to a 'how'? But this 'how' shows up the difficulty.

People, ordinary people, do not want to love. Not really. The flesh is furiously resistant to the demands of the spirit. Human beings want the end but are scared of the means, they would prefer to be handed the perfect community on a plate, hence the hankering after the 'golden age'. But this doesn't happen and, in order to give to the spirit the power to become effective in a community it must have, as any relationship must have, a symbol strong enough to focus its powers for a break-through. As in a sexual attraction, passion or 'enthusiasm' for the symbol is sparked off by the realisation of some quality in the beloved (it may be slight, or misleading) which corresponds to a real but probably unconscious need in the lover, be it an individual or a community. This symbol is usually to be embodied in a person, a real human person, who must be able, as the sexual partner is, to be the means of providing quite naturally the scope for action and extension which fulfil the demand of passion.

So far, so good. It is not difficult to find examples of such human symbols but they certainly do not seem to provide the 'answer' for which we are looking. Historically, a human leader who is effective inevitably has this double function. He must be a symbol, and as such show a perfection and completeness that does not belong to anyone 'in the flesh', and he must provide appropriate action whereby those who respond to him may discover and express their devotion. The better and more comprehensive the symbol, and the more satisfying the action which expresses it, the stronger will be the coherence and devotion of the community that is brought into being by this means, and this is not always a good thing. One need look no further than Hitler's Germany to see what can happen when symbol and action work well together. It is probably true to say that more often than not a community brought into being by such means is either dangerous and destructive or so self-enclosed as to be irrelevant to all except its own members.

And there is another pitfall awaiting this kind of community. The effective symbol for such a breakthrough must be one which can serve to renew the impulse of passion even when the emotional tide has retreated. But the symbol-character of a human being is inevitably challenged by the reality of his human limitations and, in time, these are likely to become known. In a sexual relationship the limitations of the two partners do not threaten the relatiosnhip unless it has been attached to the emotion of passion alone. Once the communication in the spirit has been made by the help of the symbol it can be continued by virtue of its intrinsic reality, for it is love which is the reality, and the personal qualities of the other person, though they may ease it or make it more difficult, are no essential barrier. The human being as he really is can never be the symbol of love, but when he is serving as a symbol, the focus of the lover's vision is so sharpened, that all but the essential quality, which corresponds to something in the lover, is excluded from immediate relevance. But the real human being is both more and less than the symbol; more because he is a whole human being and, as symbol, he is useful because of some mere accidental correspondence between himself and the unconscious needs of his lover; and less because the thing symbolised is the fullness of the self, the spirit, which is in both lover and beloved and is the perfection of both. But, afterwards, this real human being becomes, almost insensibly, the means of working out the symbol—that is, discovering the reality behind it by action which is appropriate to it. Then renewal of love comes about through sexual intercourse which is now the symbolic act of a love which is beginning to discover itself. By that time the exercise of love no longer depends on the isolating action of the sharp focus of the original vision.

But in the case of a community no such easy transition is possible. No immediate communication at the ordinary, daily level is possible between the devotees and their human symbol, and the action by which their devotion expresses itself does not lead to any closer or deeper relationship with the actual human being who initiated it. The relationship has to remain at the level of symbol only, and therefore it becomes necessary to preserve the power of the symbol by protecting the devotees from knowledge of the real human being who lies behind it (as in the code of chivalry when the 'lady' remained a symbol because no real, daily, human relationship existed to change symbol into reality). This necessity of preserving the symbol leads to the creation of an apparatus of deception. This may take the form of either a deliberate propaganda machine for the preservation and intensification of the symbol, or of the massive self-deception of the human leader himself, who must convince himself of his worthiness and validity as the focus of all this devotion. Whether sincere or insincere, the result is an increasingly unreal situation, demanding more and more extravagant claims and demonstrations of power to keep it going. This need continually to escalate the impressiveness of the symbol is the dictator's nightmare and his eventual ruin.

In some cases the community created by a human symbol of liberation collapses when events catch up with it and the claims are clearly shown to be false, like poor Joanna Southcott's messianic maternity. But often enough it survives the death of its founder, and continues to maintain itself and even to grow in spite of all disproof or failure. The popular following of the 'pseudo Baldwin' (whose real name was Bertrand de Ray) continued to believe in this Messiah of the poor and to await his return, long after the imposter had fled, abandoning his claims, and had been publicly hanged at Lille in 1225. The degree to which such a community is able to continue as a reality and not merely as a habit depends on the degree to which the kind of behaviour to which the symbol impelled its devotees corresponds to at least some of the real needs of human nature—though human beings can disregard certain aspects of themselves for a surprisingly long time, provided the assurance of liberation or salvation by this means is strong and consistent. The extreme puritanical sects are an obvious example of this ability to suppress large areas of what is usually regarded as normal living.

If Christianity can be shown to have fallen into the trap of departmentalising human life then Christianity has, in the end, failed. And the accusation that it has failed, for just this reason, must be met. The history of Christianity shows, as might be expected, much the same features as any other movement that is initiated by one person. It was begun by focusing on Christ as the symbol of liberation from the flesh. It discovered and expressed its identity in the action of mutual service, brotherly love, and renewed itself by symbolic actions which referred back to this love. This is what all communities 'of the spirit' must do. But the flesh manages often enough to deflect the impulse of the spirit in a way that accords with its own demands, and so, instead of being overcome, the rule of the flesh is consolidated. This is the 'hypocrisy' to which I referred in the last chapter. It was and is well-known in the history of Christianity, and since hypocrisy is aimed, at least implicitly, at impressing other people it expresses itself typically in institutional corruption. This occurs even though these very institutions may have been sincerely intended to be at the service of the spirit. Hypocrisy (whether in State or

Church) departmentalises, because the truth can only be known by man in his wholeness, and if he is kept in a state of internal division he cannot easily see through the deception. So hypocrisy works by using the external organisation of the community (the Law) to impose fake standards which claim to be spiritual. Thus the Roman Curia was able to consolidate power 'in the flesh' by demanding obedience as due 'in the spirit'. At the same time it strives to exclude one side or another of human nature, a side which is presented as being incompatible with the spirit which it claims to serve. Hence, in the Roman Church, exclusive emphasis on obedience, at the expense of personal honesty.

To quote Erich Fromm once more:

'Man [in an industrialised society] does not only sell commodities, he sells himself and feels himself to be a commodity. The manual labourer sells his physical energy; the business man, the physician, the clerical employee, sell their 'personality'. They have to have a 'personality' if they are to sell their products or services. This personality should be pleasing, but besides that its possessor should meet a number of other requirements: he should have energy, initiative, this, that, or the other, as the particular position may require. As with any other human commodity it is the market which decides the value of these human qualities, yes, even their very existence. If there is no use for the qualities a person offers, he *has* none . . . Thus, the self-confidence, the 'feeling of self', is merely an indication of what others think of the person. It is not *he* who is convinced of his value regardless of popularity and his success on the market.'

This passage refers to values imposed by an industrial system—'market' values—but the remarks apply equally well to any organisation, including a religious one, that demands a special type of behaviour, a special set of qualities of its members, as necessary to the salvation it offers.

It is precisely this kind of hypocrisy, with its arbitrary moulding of human life, which has bedevilled Christianity as it has inevitably undermined and destroyed other idealistic systems of thought. The 'falsity' of the apparently good standards imposed consists in their incompleteness. They do not correspond with the human need for wholeness, they are not rooted in the essential self which is the guarantor of reality—that is, of what is 'good' for man. If this tendency to divide and distort were really of its essence, Christianity could only be discarded with relief, though perhaps with gratitude for past achievements in the flesh. But if these tendencies can be shown to be the natural reaction of 'the world' and 'the flesh' (in which Christianity must be and work) to an unprecedented attack on its achievements then the matter demands further consideration.

A few pages back (120-2) I gave a paraphrase of part of a dialogue between Christ and some of his would-be followers, as reported in the gospel of John. In it, Christ claimed to be the spokesman of the authentic human spirit, one who could be validated by the response to him of that spirit itself. He claimed to be essentially connected to and aware of this core of human life, and to be its link with the everyday realities of food and work. But he went on to offer himself as the symbol and means of liberation, yet refused to assume the finality of it in himself. He gave them a sign, and the sign was himself, but himself as essentially for them. This sign was not merely for them as individuals but for them in the sharing of the new life they were to discover by means of him. This life is described elsewhere as the 'light' by which people know each other and are made one in that knowledge. It is this offering of himself as essentially for them, for the creation and extension of the life of the spirit in and between them, that he expressed by referring to himself as their 'food'. He is, he suggests, the symbol which will not fail them, as other human symbols have failed them and will fail them, because the actions that commitment to himself demands belong to the very nature of being human. It draws into itself all the powers and levels of human living, both individual and communal, so that these two act as one and there is no conflict. The relationship in the spirit, established by the focusing power of himself as symbol, is a relationship between the members of the community of which he is, simply, the 'mediator'.

This becomes clear from his own words, or rather the words in which the first Christians passed on his essential message. They are reported at the end of that momentous dialogue of which I used a part to explain the nature of the problem to which Christ claimed to be the solution. But in trying to convey clearly the meaning of this crucial statement it is not always useful to employ the precise terms of the original record because they have lost their original effectiveness as communication. This has happened through the inevitable historical process of distortion brought about by the sustained though generally unconscious hypocrisy of religious people. They were trying, as we all do, to eat their cake and have it, or, in Christ's own words, to 'serve two masters'.

The claim which Christ made, and which was accepted by the Church which he founded, is one which, it seems, must be made in some form if there is to be any way out of the impasse of the conflicting claims of the individual and the community. The alternative is to decide that the impasse is real and not merely apparent. In that case all we can do is to continue to live in the world and the flesh as best we may, and for as long as we can manage to do so without letting the force of the spirit blow up the whole structure from within. The threat of nuclear destruction that hangs over us is not only the final physical result of failure to resolve this conflict, it is also the symbol of the conflict itself, and a living and inescapable proof of what man is prepared to do to himself when the power of the spirit is not used, but suppressed until the point is reached when internal pressure is no longer equalised by external control.

But the idea of indefinite containment in a state of unresolved tension is the only answer that many people can give, and those who do so can only do it honestly if they have fully realised the force of the claim that the impasse is not a real one. In effect, then, this is what Christ said about himself, and Christianity stands or falls by this claim:

'I am that thing which human nature needs if it is to develop in any way which is proper to it; therefore anyone who is willing to take what I give will not remain unsatisfied, and he who commits himself to me will find his desires fulfilled. I know very well that many people will see me, a human being, and find in that nothing to compel commitment. But those who are responsive to what is authentic in themselves will give me a hearing, and anyone who goes as far as that will find nothing in me to force him to turn away again. This is because I live by the life of the spirit, that which is the core of human nature and desires to be set free, and I am putting this essential life into terms of life as you know it, life in the flesh, not because I need to do so, for myself, but because the life of the spirit demands this, since its very nature is to be shared. And it is of the nature of this life that it should include all that belongs to being human, it rejects nothing but can, in the end, transform the whole. This is what the spirit in man is bound to do—to achieve a final wholeness by means of the commitment of love to other human beings in their condition as they actually are. Commitment to me in this sense can bring about wholeness and liberation from within.'

The objection of most of his original hearers to ideas of this kind were those that he expected and had foretold. They looked at him, a human being like another, confined by time and place and social situation like anyone else, and they openly derided his claim to know more about the way to wholeness and freedom than their own well-tested and established religious leaders. In his attempt to break through the barrier of incomprehension he pushed language to the very limit of its power and beyond. In so doing he forged a symbol which was as old as it was new and has gathered into itself the essence of his message and transmitted it at so many different levels of meaning and relevance that it is literally inexhaustible, and even retains its value for those who reject the conviction that he expressed by it. Translated as before, inadequately but necessarily, he developed, or rather intensified, the message in this way:

'It is no use complaining because you can't make sense of what I'm telling you. No one can possibly understand unless he has come to realise in himself the existence of the same authentic self which is what I live by. But if he does recognise the source of my power he will be able to share it and achieve wholeness by it. Your religious teachers have always told you that it was possible to know and learn from this hidden self which makes you human. Everyone who has learnt this recognises me. Not that you can normally have any direct experience of this hidden self—only one who is in conscious touch with it could be said to know his essential self—but I tell you for certain that if you can commit yourself to me—to me as the link with what you recognise as the core of yourself—that will open up for you the way to wholeness. This is because I am the 'food' which gives strength to the spirit, so that it can grow. The old symbols of wholeness, of the perfect community, were well enough for their purpose, but they were symbols and no more. They were not able to feed the spirit, they only made ordinary life more bearable. But this 'food' really belongs to the spirit itself, so if any one can accept this sort of food he can really begin to live fully. He is on the way to wholeness, which is something that stands outside time and place. And this food which I can give you, the food which really belongs to the essential self in human beings, is myself, my own physical existence as a human being.'

It is hardly surprising that the Jews found this hard to swallow, in every sense. To excuse themselves from facing up to the real and revolutionary meaning of what he was saying they pretended to take his words in the most crude and literal way possible. 'How can this man give us himself to eat?' And Christ's reaction was to take them up at this literal level and emphasise it, as if to force them, by the sheer, ludicrous paradox of his literal meaning to make a choice: either they must reject the whole thing or they must make the unconditional response which authentic passion demands. This is what he said, and it will be seen that the attempt to translate his language into our language is driven closer and closer to his own terms, because it was the very ridiculous incomprehensibility of what he was saying that gave it its crucial importance. It was the moment of truth for those whose faith in him had been that of honest and willing hearts, uncommitted but open. Now they must choose, and still today they must choose:

'I tell you for certain that if you are not prepared to accept a literal human being of flesh and blood as you are, as the food which your very nature requires, then you will remain humanly dead. But the man who does take this human fact as his food will be really alive, and this life will come to its perfection. This is because myself, a human being of flesh and blood, is what yourself needs if it is to grow. So anyone who eats this food will discover that his life is really mine, and mine is his. Just as I live by the life which is that of the essential self in all men (and this is what makes me want to communicate it, for it is of its nature to be shared) so the man who takes me as his food will live by that same life. And this is the real bread, the food that belongs to the essence of being human. It is not the kind of food that the old religions can give you, which served only for life on the horizontal plane. This kind of bread nourishes the life which can ignore time and place and all the limitations which confine human beings.'

Even when he realised the effect these words were having on many of his hitherto devoted followers he refused to explain or soften them. He even pushed them further: 'Does this worry you? Then what would you think if you were to perceive without doubt this human individual in evident possession of the life which belongs to you all but which you cannot recognise because you are stuck in the flesh? It is the spirit which is the real life of man, but you cannot get at it by any means available to the flesh. That is why I have spoken to you in words which can give you access to the spirit which is your real life. But some of you won't believe this.'

He was right. They didn't, and they don't. He did not blame them then, and he made it clear that it was quite unnecessary for him to pronounce any kind of judgment on them. The proof of his words would come from themselves, by their effect in relation to the nature of their own very self, which they were rejecting in rejecting him.

Some did not, at this point, reject him. But if they stayed with him it was not because they understood what he was getting at. It is obvious that they had no idea what he meant. They stayed because they recognised in him their link with a fundamental reality in themselves. They were prepared to accept him and let this reality grow and illuminate the whole of life. It was not a light for the intellect only, though eventually the intellect would share in this light which, in Christ's own way of thinking, is the same thing as life—the eternal life of the spirit, the Kingdom of Heaven.

This extraordinary speech is the beginning of all Christian ideas about the relationship between the spirit and the world, the needs of the individual and of the community. This community aspect becomes much clearer in another discourse which is presented as given specially to those whom he had chosen to begin the work of trying to put his ideas into practice. But already the outlines of his solution are clear enough. The symbol that focuses the impulse towards freedom is himself. He is a man, a flesh-and-blood human being, and therefore the action which is appropriate for the expression and development of this impulse must be directed towards other human beings, as human, in their concrete situation. ('Whatever you did to the least of my brothers you did to me.') But there must be a means of renewing the impulse of the spirit and clarifying its meaning, and this (psychologically equivalent for the community to the sexual encounter of a couple) is provided by the aspect of himself which he refers to as 'food'. Food gives life, but it is a shared life, a common life, and the sharing of food has always been seen as an assertion of community. ('I could eat you' has also become almost a cliché of lovers' talk.) And this 'food' which is himself is one which is necessary to the life of the essential self, a life which is not private but ultimately shared whether we like it or not. But the spirit cannot realise the fact that it is not really, but only apparently, bound by the shell of particular personality except by 'coming out' in response to an exterior demand. This demand is the one Christ makes, and he makes it as a human being, for the sake of other human beings. The levels of meaning which are to be found and have been found in this central symbol are as many as the people who have looked for meaning. At one end of the scale are those who see the food-symbol in terms of something near to primitive magic notions that, in another form, make sense of cannibalism. At the other end are those who can appreciate the intelligible human meaning of this, can also take in a devotion of personal admiration and love for Christ the historical man and, on his instructions, can pour out the passionate love that he demands on any and every human thing that requires it. In doing this they realise that it is this simultaneous receiving and giving which is the real 'food' of community in the spirit, just as the sexual encounter is the 'food' of mutual love between an individual man and woman. To this the outward gesture which Christians make in the liturgical assembly—the Breaking of Bread—has the same relevance as the strictly physical gestures of lovemaking have to the exchange of love. The two (the gesture and the love it expresses) are essentially connected, but can be separated, and often are, sometimes for good, sometimes for ill.

The Christian solution to the individual-versus-community problem, then, is the attempt to transform social relationships from within. It does not require the abandonment of the institutions of a civilised society. On the contrary, it commands respect for them, as the necessary means for the continued existence and sanity of man in the flesh, but it regards them as essentially temporary. Being general, such codes and structures can never do more than approximate to the needs of the individual, and we should therefore try to establish them on the basis of 'freedom *from*' rather than 'freedom *to*'. 'Freedom to' belongs properly to the realm of the spirit. Only the spirit can discover what it truly needs and a 'freedom' which is not authentically of the spirit will be evil, destructive and disintegrating, since it will carry the prestige of the 'spiritual' without its realism and essential honesty. Many strong religious or social movements have tried to impose this 'freedom to' in the name of the spirit, for the desire for a short cut to freedom is always present, and hypocrisy creates the illusion of the spiritual which can be so plausible and attractive in such movements. Manicheism finds its adherents in every age, and communism also appeals strongly to the spiritual ambitions of man. Actual, present day communism in practice is busy trying to clear up the mess made by earlier insistence on 'freedom to . . .' without sacrificing the power of the symbol of freedom.

But the gospel message insists on patience and steady growth. The fruit will not form if we stunt or starve or distort the growing tree. 'By their fruits you will know them' and the fruits of the authentic human spirit are recognisable immediately. Meanwhile, for the Christian, the physical gesture of the Breaking of Bread is a sort of test of the authenticity of social relationships. As a human gesture it is so obvious and simple that it has nothing to offer to the pretensions of hypocrisy. Hence, perhaps, the desire to dress it up in esoteric symbolism. It implies so clearly the obligation to share life as we share bread that it is necessary to distort its meaning in order to ignore its implied reproach. This prosaic gesture of sharing food is an acceptance of Christ's claim that in this action we are professing the desire, at least, to become what we essentially are: for the sake of what is at the heart of the fact of our humanness we must accept all the unknown dangers and pains that the search for it must involve. Moreover we are making this profession simply on the strength of Christ's promise, because we recognise that he really does speak for the most fundamental reality in each one. But this gesture is also the assertion of the fact that wholeness and truth can only be achieved in a shared life, so that the community of love which passion establishes between two must be realised also in the wider community, not as a mass, but each by each, by the symbol and the work and the physical gesture and the final, dynamic reality which we call love.

For those who reject the Christian claim there are, it seems, two alternatives. Some means must be found of establishing a community which is authentically human at the level of the spirit, and which must, therefore, fulfil the psychological conditions required by the nature of such a community. Or the possibility of such a community in the spirit must be denied and the hope of wholeness abandoned as an illusion and a distraction. There remain the achievements of civilisation, and they are not small. There remain also individual pleasures and hopes and sorrows, acts of love and courage and companionship and compassion. These can continue even under the shadow of futility and in a tunnel marked 'no exit', and by doing so compel admiration and respect. But I cannot help wondering whether those who accept this very beautiful human pessimism and live by it, often heroically, are not, unconsciously, living on borrowed capital. The hope they consciously reject is perhaps still working, still feeding their courage and humour. The spirit of Christ is often easily recognisable in those who deny all knowledge of him, as he himself once said. So the believer and the unbeliever can find themselves, whether they like it or not, in the same dark tunnel. It really is the same one, not just a similar one, and if they keep on going (as many do not) the reaction of both seems to be basically the same, whether expressed in words or in living. It is a very old cry, but always new for the human being who, surrounded by a fog of impenetrable futility and the certainty of death, has the crazy courage to say, 'Though he slay me, yet will I trust him', and go on trying to be human.

CHAPTER VI

'THE LAST SHALL BE FIRST'
Upside-down morality

PASSION, in some form or other, is that which makes the first breaks in that structure of careful human compromises which is the laborious, intricate and admirable architecture of the flesh. But the working out of its commitment takes place very largely in terms of the codes and customs of the Law, though the motive power is different. The Law means, to condense previous explorations of this concept, the total public relevance of a 'way of life'—the external rules, customs, laws, and standards of behaviour that control behaviour from the outside and determine how people think of themselves. But these moral-political-social codes of 'the world' are only generalised approximations to the human truth of which passion gives a glimpse. Sooner or later the person who has responded to the demand that passion makes begins to discover that the approximation is simply inadequate. While prepared to grant its usefulness, even its absolute necessity, he must cease to argue for it from an *a priori* position but must look at the human situation in its particularity. The study of moral situations which follows is necessarily concerned almost entirely with subjective experiences, and must run the risk of remaining incomprehensible, even when concrete examples and experiences are used as markers. It is worth the attempt, all the same, because the question of moral ambiguity is fundamental to the search for humanness.

Once the inadequacy of even the best codes as tools of the spirit is realised it becomes clear that the general enforcement of principles, however good, must be disastrous. When they can be made to work well they do so by a system of evasions and adjustments, sometimes conscious (which is casuistry) but more often unconscious. In the rare cases where one man or group has had the power to enforce a principle in all its force the result has invariably been horrible, and the more directly such a principle is concerned with the shaping of personal conscience the more horrible have been the results. Some of the worst atrocities in history have been perpetrated in the name of religious truth and in particular of Christian truth. Of many possible examples, I quote only three: the notorious Inquisition, the Covenanters, and the rule of the Puritan Fathers in New England.

This is inevitable, because principles which are purely political or social, while they may work out unjustly and even cruelly, are concerned solely with the external behaviour of human beings. Therefore those who are prepared to conform externally can continue, though perhaps uncomfortably, to live and try to discover themselves. But a principle which is concerned with the nature of man cannot rest content with touching behaviour alone, it is bound to seek in behaviour the evidence of a direction of conscience, and thereby to attempt to reach and coerce the central fortress of personality. Communism, in its first ideological fervour, is the obvious example of this. Religious principles are bound to be of this kind and ideological principles come in this category since they have, in this aspect, the same human significance as religious principles strictly so called.

The significance of this disturbing historical fact is first of all simply that the wider the application of a principle is to be, the more strictly utilitarian, external and expedient it should strive to be. But it has also a significance for the individual, when he realises that in the end even the highest moral principles may become a camouflage rather than a support, an escape from self rather than a framework within which it may be discovered.

This does not, however, set a man free from the obligation to conform to a general moral norm, provided it is one which is 'humanly shaped' and is well designed for the support and education of people who cannot yet (and perhaps never will) do without it.

St Paul insisted that a Christian who knew perfectly well that meat sacrificed to pagan gods was just like any other meat, and could therefore eat it without hurt to his own conscience, might still find himself obliged in charity to abstain from eating it. He must do this for the sake of those of his brethren who could not rid themselves of the emotional associations of their pagan origins and would therefore be troubled at the idea of eating sacrificed meat, an action which would seem to be a compromise with old and rejected ways. The Christian who, in the arrogance of his own enlightenment, insisted on his right to eat any meat he pleased would be putting an obstacle in the way of his brother's personal development. Therefore the enlightened one was under an obligation to respect his brother's irrational emotional reactions, and to make his own conduct conform to its requirements. If he would not do so he simply demonstrated that his enlightenment was not the 'light' that Christ intended, which is something to be shared, but only a self-glorification, and as such a dead end, since the self can only discover itself in relation.

This must be said, but saying it does not provide an excuse for evasion of the personal responsibility for achieving an authentic morality, and it is at the level of immediate application that the external moral norm can and probably will come into conflict with the demands of the authentic self. In the last resort the personal conscience must be given priority, because public 'knowing' is inevitably solely concerned with what is fully conscious, whereas personal self-knowledge must deal with, though it cannot express, the unconscious area of living. Only a whole response to situations, one including the unconscious area in human life, can therefore be said to be authentic or 'spiritual'.

But decisions contrary to an accepted norm are bound to run the risk of being made for reasons irrelevant to the true needs of the spirit, perhaps out of a desire for singularity, as an assertion of personal independance, as an act of rebellion or revenge, or as philosophical rationalisations of mere inclination. How can we distinguish between the authentic 'no' that springs from the realisation that conformity with the Law means the abdication of personal responsibility, and the sham refusal, the gesture whose real purpose is not to discover the spirit but to protect the flesh from the legitimate discipline of the Law by which it grows?

It is not possible simply to judge by results because we inevitably rationalise our opinion of the results to accord with our moral preconceptions. So a man like Thomas More who sticks to an unpopular principle may be canonised as a martyr by some and condemned as a suicidal fool by others. One man whose unorthodox ideas 'work out'—a Wilberforce or a Lawrence—will be acclaimed as a pioneer by a generation that has modified its norm to accommodate his. Another no more eccentric experimenter will seem merely laughable and his followers pathetic or comic characters, and so the whole abortive movement will eventually drop out of history. The nineteenth-century German 'Nazarene' group of monk-artists are almost forgotten, but their enthusiasm was as dedicated as that of the Impressionists. The medieval alchemists' pursuit of an esoteric truth is generally both misrepresented and derided. Yet their learning was both deep and—in historical perspective—remarkably perceptive.

We cannot even read the results backwards and say that an authentic decision will be the result of a life lived according to obviously high moral standards, because again we are imposing on the situation our own accepted ideas of what 'high moral standards' must be. So we are bewildered when, for instance, a loose-living young woman is prepared to risk death and endure torture for the sake of a cause. We are scandalised when a high-principled, obviously good, kind and courageous person slips with apparent ease into conformity with the demands of, for instance, a political ideology which is manifestly opposed to his declared principles. We may suggest, in the first case, that the challenge of heroism brought out the submerged 'best' in the girl, and in the second that the situation produced a type of pressure which played on the particular weakness of the man and caused him to abandon his principles. But if the girl had continued to sleep around and had eventually been killed in a car crash, and if the man, unharassed, had proceeded in his high-minded way to his life's end, what would be the normal judgment on them? Would anyone stop to wonder whether the girl's behaviour was perhaps

due basically to an insatiable urge to discover something real—
although a desire unsupported by the things that make it possible
to do this without losing one's moral or psychological balance?
Do we ask ourselves sufficiently often to what extent conformity
with (perfectly good) moral principles can be an escape from
personal responsibility?

One of the things which has been done by certain contemporary
novelists is to make this kind of moral ambiguity a matter which
the public conscience is obliged to take seriously. The forceful
presentation of the freedom which comes from honestly facing up
to the implications of this central and ineradicable uncertainty
about the moral value of particular actions is one of the important developments which has taken place in the moral sphere
in this generation. Perceptive writers have noted it throughout
the history of literature, but it is only comparatively recently
that the full implications of this could be publicly canvassed—and
accepted.

But this freedom only has meaning within the framework of
the Law, for it is in relation to the Law that it can be appreciated
as freedom. It is a freedom which makes it possible to make
authentic decisions not in defiance of the Law but in conscious
relation to it, even if in opposition to its demands. This is possible
only through the acceptance of the fact of central uncertainty.
This uncertainty takes away the support which we normally seek
from implicit public approval, based on some recognisable
moral value in the decision made. The unnerving realisation that
we are not in a position to have any such interior moral certainty
sweeps away all the ego-directed motives and leaves only the
naked desire for personal truth. We can never be sure whether
a decision was good or not, in itself, for the conditions that made
it necessary are found to be subject to the same moral ambiguity,
and the results cannot be tied down to it by a chain of clear cause
and effect. In this moral vacuum authentic moral decisions can be
made, and probably in this only, though the means by which such
a 'vacuum' is created will vary from one case to the next according
to the historical-ideological setting.

By realising this moral isolation it is possible to appreciate, and when possible conform to, the Law, but to do so 'in the spirit' because now the Law no longer carries the coercive emotional force which it must have so long as it is functioning as an educational tool.

Such an unsupported decision must, nevertheless, have a direction, or there will be no purpose to guide the decision. Ultimately, it can only be directed by the conviction that one's own self demands this, though the decision may run in a direction clean contrary to inclination, or even to reason and common sense. There must be very few decisions of this kind—perhaps many people never make one at all—for most moral choices are straight-forward decisions in which the element of real indecision is so small that it would be hard to say whether they were strictly choices at all. Education or inclination or circumstances have virtually made the decision in advance.

This is inevitable and necessary, but it is also inevitable that those who do commit themselves to the search for authenticity (or 'freedom' or personal wholeness or whatever pretentious phrase one is obliged to use in order to make the intention clear) will eventually realise the need for decisions which are authentic. But then the temptation is to assert the importance of one's individuality by denying the relevance of the demands of other people or of the Law, as if authenticity were only to be found in isolation. The assertion of the personal self against others seems the obvious way of securing oneself from dishonest concessions to the Law or the pressure of emotional commitments. I am not you and, if I am to discover myself, I must distinguish myself from you or I shall lose the sense of myself. From this springs the conviction that in order to make an authentic choice one must be able to feel one's identity as involved in the choice, asserting itself against the influences which would disintegrate it. Typically, this occurs in adolescence when the need to discover one's identity makes personal assertion necessary. It is necessary to know oneself as distinct before it is possible to begin discovering the essential thing which this self is. If this is not done real commitment is impossible because the person remains always spiritually a child—good and happy, perhaps, but firmly within the comforting enclosure of 'home', which is the Law.

But the assertion of self is the beginning, not the end. The essential self-discovery can only be made in relation, which is another way of saying that what we are can only be known by what we do. But this need for self-assertion can push the personality off the road of search for authenticity and into a dead end. The compulsion to assert oneself as distinct and independent sometimes has to be enormously strong if it is to succeed in overcoming the factors which undermine self-confidence, such things as physical weakness or ugliness, financial or academic failure, inability to make or keep friends or personal or national humiliation (such as produced the existentialist reaction in post-war France)—in fact any of the things that make people doubt their personal value. The strength of the act of self-assertion needed in cases like this is so great that it can use up all the spiritual energy of the person, so that he can go no further at that time. Having, by this huge effort, become convinced of himself and his ultimate and indestructible self-hood, he finds himself in a void, for the very strength of the impulse has thrust away all that linked him to other people.

The real search for authenticity cannot stop there. The moral vacuum of authentic decision does not consist in a rejection of normal morality but in the recognition of a radical agnosticism in relation to it—an inability to know what is right in any but an approximate and inadequate way. Another word for this is humility. The final, searing loneliness in which such a decision must be made is not the self-created isolation of rejection but only an acknowledgement of the facts. I am not able to do things which are certainly right. If I obey the Law I shall at least be acceptable and reasonably safe, but I shall not know what I meant when I did it. If I do not obey I shall know what I meant, but I shall not know what I am, I shall have no sense of myself. But, in either case, I can have no assurance of the value of what I do.

There is only one criterion of authenticity, and that is the way in which my decision brings me into a relation of truth with another person. This is a matter of experience. The kind of behaviour which makes us feel of a person that he or she is really good is behaviour to which external standards or personal emotional satisfaction are clearly irrelevant. They are not irrelevant because such behaviour contradicts either, but because it is not motivated by either. It is the result of openness that is not so much un-selfish, in the popular sense of going against its inclinations, as simply loving, in the sense which I described earlier in the book. There is no other word for it, and it is rare enough to be recognis-able at a glance, but it is not at all a simple thing to identify in one's own behaviour, and this is the weakness of those moralists who are content to tell people that the only criterion of morality should be lovingness. So it should, but we have to be certain that we know what love is. 'Love is a direction' (it is more than that, but it is that) and this means that it is not something we can ever possess or be sure of. It is, paradoxically, true to say that we are likely to be moving in the direction of love in inverse proportion to our awareness of loving.

Most of the time we have to get along with map-symbols and signposts and rough sketch-maps of love. We need these and would be foolish to suppose we can or should do without them, but the map is not the country, the symbol is not the reality. The map and the symbol give the security of being able to identify precisely what we are looking for. The reality in either case is the place we live in, it is our 'being' and therefore not identifiable by us from the outside. This is the reason for the ambiguity of authentic moral choices. They are concerned with what we are, and what we are is in relation. What distinguishes is what separates, therefore the things that separate—'the flesh', 'the world', and 'the Law' which caters for both—can be relevant to authentic or 'loving' choices only in the sense that they are the inescapable conditions with which any choice has to deal, both as material for making a decision and for working out its implications afterwards.

The search for authenticity can never be easy and its chief enemy is the unwillingness to expose oneself to unpopularity or personal regret. This is naturally most likely to be a strong influence in the life of a person who is successful, well-behaved, has many friends and is generally approved of not only by others but by himself. This is at the back of the insistence in the gospels on the danger of riches and respectability and the advantage of being poor and neglected and even sinful. The well-to-do, either materially or psychologically, have a lot to lose. The poor in spirit are likely to be also the outwardly poor, either financially or morally or both, because these have already lost most of the things that make the acceptance of a moral vacuum difficult. The 'publicans and harlots' will go into the Kingdom of Heaven before the well-behaved, not because they are 'humble' in the usual sense that they suppose themselves to be 'bad', but because they know that they are cut off from being 'good' in any recognisable sense, and have therefore less motive for being anything but honest with themselves.

This upside-down morality is in fact rooted in the Christian understanding of the search for freedom.

It is asserted in the account of the very outset of Christ's preaching career, when John the Baptiser, recognising his cousin's outstanding goodness, saw no sense in baptising him as a sign of repentance. But Jesus insisted, saying that this sign of a change of heart was 'fitting' in order to 'fulfil all righteousness'. In other words, in order to discover the fundamental 'spiritual' wholeness which alone can 'fulfil' (i.e. make sense of the outward pattern of behaviour), something must 'happen' to a person in his inmost self and the rite of baptism is a symbol of this happening. And the evangelists associate this act of deliberately 'starting from the beginning' with the manifestation of the spirit by which Christ recognised the nature of his mission. The Kingdom of Heaven was to be preached by somebody who had deliberately associated himself with all those who recognised their radical unheavenliness. But he did not do this as a gesture to show that he sympathised, from outside, or just to encourage others to 'repent', he did it out of an utterly clear knowledge that authenticity starts with a recognition of the irrelevance to the search for freedom of all one's external actions, however good and noble. This is perfectly compatible with the insistence on exterior actions as the essential *test* of authentic morality, as I suggested earlier.

The upside-down morality of the gospels scandalised Christ's contemporaries and bewildered his followers then and since. He demanded practical charity as a *sine qua non* of membership in his Kingdom, but made friends, for preference, with people who were social parasites. He said they needed him because they were 'sinners', and so they were, but in his own estimation the Scribes and Pharisees were much greater sinners. The sinners he associated with were not people to whom he had come to 'do good' but people whose obvious moral incompetence gave them a head start in the search for freedom on which he, who was 'going to the Father', was himself engaged. They could understand what he said because so many of the barriers to communication were already down. The usual interpretation of this eccentric preference is that Christ associated with these people because they were prepared to acknowledge their sinfulness and try to do better, whereas the respectable saw no need for repentance. This is only partly true. The 'sinners' did acknowledge their sins, but not, as most of us do, as a series of actions which are repudiated as unworthy of one's better self. They knew they were sinners in the sense that they were so penetrated with the negative 'not being' of sin that they were not capable of doing 'right' as most people understand it. And in this moral wilderness they found Christ, who had entered it deliberately, whereas they had been thrown there by circumstances.

But, for most people, Christianity still appears to be *par excellence* the religion of codes; it is therefore necessary to stress how, in fact, the sense of the moral ambiguity of human actions is at the root of New Testament thinking.

The most famous of all the gospel sayings, the group known as the 'Beatitudes', contain moral paradoxes of an extreme kind. The very first one proclaims the blessedness of those who are 'poor in spirit'. One might expect that any other kind of poverty might be helpful to the freeing of the spirit. Financial or social or physical or intellectual deprivation could conceivably assist humility and detachment and have been frequently embraced by religious people for this reason. But when we remember that the 'spirit' refers to what is most real and essential in human beings the idea that Christ is recommending poverty of spirit seems fantastic. 'Poverty' means deprivation, loneliness, abandonment, utter powerlessness. It is this, as a state of the human spirit, that Christ makes the condition of 'blessedness'—that is, 'happiness'. Other phrases expand and particularise this basic idea. Blessedness is to be attributed to those who sorrow, who are helpless, who are persecuted. Blessed also are those who are 'hungry and thirsty for goodness', and this is another way of saying the same thing, for only those who are painfully aware of a lack can be said to be 'hungry and thirsty'. But the emphasis is different, for this image links up with the idea of search which is so evident throughout the gospels.

The same theme recurs in the command to 'give alms in secret', and the secrecy is to be such that 'the left hand must not know what the right hand is doing'. Real love is unaware of itself, lacks the certainty or satisfaction of conscious right-doing. 'And your Father, who sees in secret, will reward you', for this is the way to personal authenticity and that is its *only* reward, a bleak one from the point of view of the flesh, and yet self-evidently worthwhile to those who have discovered it.

It would require an entire New Testament commentary to bring out fully the upside-down morality of the Christian message. It is summed up in such famous phrases as 'the last shall be first'and 'it is easier for a camel to pass through the needle's eye than for the rich man to enter the Kingdom of God'. It is set out in stories like that of the wedding feast, to which the invited guests would not come because they had better and more immediately important things to do, so the table was filled with tramps and beggars, some of whom were not even invited but simply fetched.

It is this need for the recognition of moral incompetence that makes the impact of the Christian message much stronger and more immediate on communities or individuals who are deprived of some or all of the things that make life comfortable. And this is why it can seem reasonable to conclude that the Christian message can only have meaning in such circumstances. It is one of the reasons put forward for regarding Christianity as irrelevant to Western society as we know it, and this is an objection which is certainly valid. Christianity really is irrelevant to a community or an individual living successfully in the flesh. Only those who allow themselves to be aware of the incompleteness of life in the flesh will begin to look for something else.

The recognition of the futility of one's achievements and aims and the whole structure of one's life is so frightening that it is no wonder that one of the main streams of modern philosophy is directed to making this recognition appear unnecessary, a surrender to unreason and personal anarchy. Yet this recognition is precisely what is involved in the metanoia of which sexual passion is the type.

There is no getting away from it if one is a Christian, and many who are not Christians are increasingly unable to avoid noticing that the road to complete humanness is by way of a leap into total darkness. And both, in their confrontation with their own helplessness, can perhaps draw some small comfort from the sense of companionship, even though it is an unseen one.

The nature of the personal dilemma involved is shown not only in the words in which the evangelists proclaim Christ's message but even more emphatically in the report of his own behaviour. The agony which he had to endure in complete isolation, because his friends could not even begin to comprehend what was the matter with him, was not merely the mortal fear of imminent torture and death but the much more fundamental fear that these things represented: the horror of futility, of failure and powerlessness, the death of hope. The clue to the situation lies in his own words: the spirit is willing, but the flesh is weak. The intricate loveliness of the flesh could no longer serve the needs of the spirit, as it had done, but it struggled desperately against the disintegration which alone could give the spirit complete freedom. Being true to the authentic self demanded behaviour which involved betraying the hopes and longings of thousands. It was the end of all obvious usefulness or achievement, it must bring humiliation and despair to those who loved him best. It could easily have been avoided, and common affection, charity and the hope of long-term effectiveness all demanded that it should be avoided. It is no wonder that many sympathetic readers of the gospels (such as Shaw) have concluded that for all the beauty and clarity of his moral teaching Christ eventually succumbed to the strain and suffered a mental breakdown, so that his work ended in a messy, lunatic and unnecessary failure from which his followers, to comfort themselves, evolved a myth that could be made to account for the whole thing in terms of their own religious symbolism.

But a closer reading of the gospels would have shown that Christ himself was fully aware of the choice and what it involved. The psychological collapse which can occur in such a situation seems to be the result of giving up and trying to run away, but doing so at a point beyond the safety margin. The person can then no longer find safety in the rationally mapped regions of the flesh. Aimless and terrified, he cannot accept his helplessness but seizes hold of any fantasy that offers a hand grip. This seems to be a possible reason for the collapse of personality that occurs in cases of successful brain-washing, so that the 'new' personality can then easily be imposed. It was in Gethsemane that Christ came closest to this point. He wanted to run away. The flesh was no longer any support to him, and the human friendship to which he appealed in desperation was, he soon realised, of no use in this essentially solitary struggle. He wanted, as we all do, to find some means of reconciling the demands of the 'I'—the clear goodness and worthwhileness of conscious human living—with the obscure claims of the need for personal authenticity. Most of the time, for most people, a compromise is not only possible but essential and right. But in the last resort there is a choice, and Christ made it, because in the end he realised that there was no way out except forward. 'Not as "I" want it, but as *you* demand it', and the 'you' is first of all the essential and authentic self, because this is 'where' people find truth if there is such a thing; here and nowhere else. Whatever else may be attributed to or predicated of this basic reality in human life, this is still the essential point of it as far as human beings are concerned.

Having made the choice, Christ was able to go on to the end. One of the odd and at first sight inexplicable things about the passion narrative is the sort of relaxed and easy attitude of a man whom one would expect to be almost unbearably 'strung up' to meet such an ordeal. But his attention was obviously on the people around him and not on himself.

This is the last stage in the search for authenticity or wholeness of the self, or life 'in the spirit', or whatever one wants to call it. At this stage the irrelevance of conscious, exterior moral standards is obvious. But if it is inescapable at this point it cannot therefore be regarded as something that is of concern only to those who are driven into a corner by circumstances. This moral vacuum is present at the heart of all real choices, even those made according to the Law, and taking into account the legitimate demands of the flesh. The whole paradox of people who must live in the world and the flesh and yet are bound to seek there the way to the life of the spirit is perhaps best presented in the peculiar story of the unjust steward, a story whose meaning has baffled and bewildered Christian apologists for centuries.

The first thing to notice about this story is that it is a funny story. The style of the thing, the details of the steward's interviews with successive debtors, show the typical build-up of the tale designed to make people laugh, and the sudden let-down of the moral volte-face in the last line is a normal humorist's trick. Almost the whole story is on a consistent moral plane. It is about a thorough rogue who has no higher standard than his own worldly comfort. Knowing Christ's other stories, and the high value he put on service of other people, it seems inevitable that something very unpleasant will happen to the steward to show him that all his worldly forethought was useless and wrong. But the Master in the story, who had been cheated and defrauded all the way through, 'commended the dishonest steward for his prudence'.

The expected and desired dramatic climax of retribution is twitched away and the emotional pitch of expectation finds nothing to satisfy it. The result of pricking a moral balloon of this kind is to make people release their pent-up emotions in laughter, and the laugh is on them. But the funniness of the story is not merely peripheral, a trick to make people remember it. The moral let-down is the whole purpose of the story, it shows up by its central paradox a whole philosophy of life, and explains this quite clearly in the little commentary that follows the story. It is the key to the apparent contradiction in so much of Christ's teaching, which at one moment demands practical charity as the condition of belonging to the Kingdom of Heaven, and at another insists that no good works are any qualification for it and that socially useless people are nearer to it than the law-abiding.

The terms in which the little commentary explains this story are clear enough, but its relevance to that central dilemma of normal life which so greatly exercises the minds of this generation can perhaps be appreciated more exactly if it is expanded in the terms which I have used to discuss the question so far.

The Master in the story commends the 'dishonest steward', and the adjective is unequivocal. The story does not suggest that the steward was 'not really' dishonest. He really was thoroughly dishonest, and yet commendable. The steward's dilemma is that of all human beings. We can recognise the 'rightness' of certain kinds of behaviour, we know them to be 'really' and not just expediently right. But circumstances may make it impossible to be 'honest' and still live. There are some who have the strength of personality to carve out a completely new life for themselves in which they can live their principles unhindered. They are strong enough to 'dig', as the steward was not, and so be independent of the market place of human compromise. There are some who find a way out by leaving all the decisions to other people and thus avoiding any moral dilemma, but the steward in the story is ashamed to 'beg', which is an abdication of responsibility. But why is the steward about to lose his job anyway? He has 'wasted his Master's goods'. He has not cared enough about the 'treasure' entrusted to him to use it and increase it. He has become 'poor' by squandering for his own personal benefit the capital of goodness that was in his control. In other words he has put himself in the position of the 'publicans and sinners' who have lost any claim to public—or self—respect. He discovers that he is 'poor in spirit', he is without means to achieve any kind of human value or wholeness. Only one course remains to him. He will use the credit that does not, he knows, belong to him, in order to make friends. The gratitude of his master's debtors for relieving a little the burden of their debt will make them glad to take him in even when he has nothing else to recommend him. There is even a hint that their 'gratitude' might be activated by a little blackmail.

His Master commended him for his sensible behaviour, because people who live in the flesh ('of this world') must accept this fact and not pretend that they can behave as if they were already wholly of the spirit ('of light') .The flesh is the means by which people communicate with each other; there is no other; therefore it is 'prudent' to use it for this purpose. As long as we are in a position to 'make friends' by means of the things of the flesh then we should do so, even though we know very well that they are not 'authentic', that they are at best only symbols of the reality beyond our control or apprehension. Nobody should pretend that this is ideal and that their behaviour is 'righteous'. Like the steward, they should recognise that they are making use of something which is not of the essence of human life (is not 'theirs'), but essential or not it is all they have at the moment and they had better use it 'prudently'. If they do, when a time comes when they can no longer escape the realisation of their own futility, their moral incompetence, they will still have the companionship, the communication 'in the spirit', which they have established by means of the flesh. This bond is the one real thing, it is independent of the conditions of space and time, it is an 'eternal habitation', which is always another's, as Charles Williams said.

It is therefore wrong for someone who desires freedom and wholeness to despise or neglect the immediate conditions of daily life, for although they may seem unessential they shape the development of the true, 'spiritual' self. Someone who takes trouble over the routine details of life in the flesh (although he knows it is 'dishonest' or 'inauthentic') is likely to be able to face up honestly to the greater demands of the spirit. The flesh is our 'home' and we have to grow up properly in it before we are fit to go out from it. If we can't and won't cope with the commerce of ordinary life we are unlikely to cope courageously with the true riches of the spirit. And if we have not got on with the business of living in the flesh, although it is not 'essential', we shall be unable to understand or respond to the demands of the essential self.

The comment in St Luke's gospel ends with the famous phrase: 'You cannot serve God and Mammon', which seems to imply a contradiction between the two, but the solution to the paradox is in the whole of the rest of the story and its moral. You cannot serve God and Mammon, but you must use Mammon in the service of God. You cannot set yourself to perfect life in the flesh and *also* to find the freedom of the spirit, but you can and must (for there is no other way) set yourself to find in the flesh the means of communication in the spirit, which is the real way to freedom for the 'poor in spirit'.

This odd story shows perhaps more clearly than any the Christian recognition of the reality of the human situation. It refuses to take a way out by denying the existence of any but immediate material concerns and the moral decisions directly and clearly involved in them. This is observably not the way to human maturity, although it may be the best (a very good best) that can be done in certain psychological conditions. But it refuses also to deny the necessity and importance of life in the flesh, even while recognising its basic 'dishonesty'.

The link between the two, the only possible link, is love, the spirit in its activity, which finds its means of growth in the symbols of the flesh and is developed by practical living in the flesh, but is in itself the 'honesty' of the spirit, which belongs to man when everything else has failed him.

CHAPTER VII

'AN ANGEL OF SATAN'

The demonic in human life

So far I have discussed the fact of the desire for freedom, the initial commitment to search for it, the nature of the early 'break-through' which I have called passion, and the conditions in which this is most likely to occur and continue to extend the life of the spirit. The life of the real self is in a true sense beyond good and evil, yet must develop in the framework of the Law. But there is a huge region of human nature which is beyond the control of the Law. It demands to be recognised and cannot be rejected with impunity. It makes itself felt most clearly when circumstances do not force people to use all their energies in the need for survival, and is therefore particularly acute in Western society now.

Our society is characterised by a sense of alienation, futility and purposelessness—literature, art and philosophy all express this awareness and the attempt to come to terms with it. It comes at the end of a long striving for liberation from material suffering and hardship, and the desire for human betterment has concentrated on these for so long that it is a bitter disillusion to find that these longed-for fruits taste of dust and ashes. It was natural to feel that once people had reasonable freedom from pain, hunger, fatigue, constricting ignorance, guilt phobias, unrealistic and harsh laws, they would no longer suffer the acute discontent that seizes on a symbol to lead it to freedom. And it was supposed that this 'freedom from' would therefore remove the need for religion, the symbol of freedom *par excellence*.

But in fact this is not what happens. As Erich Fromm shows so lucidly, we live in a society that has achieved an unprecedented freedom from poverty and sickness and oppression. We have got rid of the worst kinds of drudgery and the more obvious forms of ignorance. Our legal systems still bristle with injustices but by and large people do not feel threatened by arbitrary and unjust government. The more extreme prejudices in the realm of sexual morality have evaporated to an extent that has led people to describe the result as a sexual revolution.

The result of all this has not been an increase in contentment. The most contented people are still those who would have been contented anyway, in the absence of gross suffering—people with satisfying work to do and ability to do it. There is no observable proportion between decrease of suffering and increase of content. On the contrary, the removal of immediate anxieties seem merely to have released an enormous discontent. Those, like Nietszche, who are able to make their impulse to break out of constricting comfort explicit and intelligible to others are rare, but a less conscious version of their predicament is common enough, and it may be the basic reason for the restless mixture of cynicism, defiant pessimism and half humorous bitterness that pervades so much contemporary writing. We have achieved a condition in which release from the more immediate anxieties makes it possible to confront ourselves and discover our existence as individuals but, as I discussed in the last chapter, it is individuality in a void, with nowhere to go. And yet it still wants to go somewhere. Does this 'somewhere' exist as a real part of humanness, or is it a fantasy to distract us from the only real humanness?

The attractively puritan solution of existentialist thinking is to string across the void a series of deliberate actions which make sense in relation to each other and have some immediate purpose in relation to other individuals in their own isolation. The determination to do this and to regard it as all that can be done is a determination to arrest the process of self-discovery at this point. I say 'arrest', because it requires a deliberate decision to do so, since it is not in the nature of human desires to limit themselves in this way. They are by nature larger and vaguer, more hopeful and less defined. I am not arguing that the 'unnaturalness' of such a determination makes it wrong. It is the stubborn assertion that there is something in being human after all, when every apparent meaning in human life has faded in the light of a bright technological dawn. I am suggesting that, in order to continue to assert the sole validity of consciously chosen actions linked across the void in a garland of limited but self-made purpose, it is necessary to deny the relevance and even the existence of anything prior in human life. If a man's existence as human is his own creation and nothing else then the undifferentiated 'home' from which we distinguish ourselves must be rejected as un-human or even anti-human. There can be no compromise with it, it is the perpetual threat to man's humanity. This is the naked peak of the human ascent from the sub-human. In relation to the achievement of humanness, this region of undifferentiation must appear to be totally and irredeemably 'evil', that is opposed to the 'good' of humanness. Therefore man, insofar as he is man, is committed to constant war with it.

This looks like the final conclusion that has to be accepted as the result of the long struggle to set human beings free to be human. All the symbols that helped on the way—religion, patriotism, the image of absolute truth—all have gone, and there is left only each man in his own precarious isolation, threatened by the evil sub-human from which he came and to which he must go back.

The odd thing about this is that it is the final result of the assertion of the value of individual humanness which began with the Renaissance. We opted for whole independent man, we wanted to rid him of ignorance and disease and superstition, and we were convinced that in that way we would get rid of evil, which was only the result of ignorance, for we were sure that man is noble in himself and that it is only his limitations which prevent the discovery of his true glory. We had to reject the medieval Christian way of thinking which contrasted nature with grace, the bodily with the spiritual, the vices with the virtues, the devil with God. Having done our best to set man free from his more obvious limitations, and having succeeded to an astonishing extent (with the confident hope of further success) the final result is a return to a more profound dualism than ever Christian theologians worked out in their attempts to make the Christian paradoxes intelligible by interpreting them as contradictions. We are back where we started, with a Sartrian philosophy that rejects the 'natural' (the instinctive, the unconscious) as 'unhuman' and commits man to a life-long struggle to free himself from this original sin which vitiates all his actions. The devils of Buchenwald and Belsen lurk in the shadows of the flesh—and this flesh is not the Pauline concept but our old friend the natural body with its jungle appetites that drag man down again to sub-human level. 'There is no health in us' and we cannot even ask the Lord to have mercy on us because, being our conscious self, he is incapable of mercy. He is merely just.

So at the end of the road that began with the search for man we find ourselves face to face with the devil. The devil, as a phenomenon of human life, is the dark, untameable area of un-conscious life, but only *insofar as we are opposed to it* in our efforts to distinguish and discover ourselves.

At this point, we have two alternatives. We can accept the implications of the new dualism, we can commit ourselves to the limited but determined assertion of humanness in conscious actions unrelated except to each other. This involves war to the death with all the human implications which we are tempted to discover in what is unconscious and 'natural' in our lives—sex and love and reverence and the desire for companionship and the nostalgia that beauty creates. If we adopt this alternative such things can only be tolerated if they can be explained in terms of practical utility or residual animality, otherwise they will under-mine our will to be human in final loneliness. This philosophy has an inner coherence which is attractive to people with a passion for the verifiable, because it puts the essence of humanness indisput-ably within our grasp. There is very little of it, but what there is we can manage, if we have courage enough. But it can only claim allegiance if we are prepared to accept its own definition of itself. If the same facts and states of mind are looked at from a different point of view they look different, therefore the other alternative is to realise the importance of the fact that people do seek this hard and desperate kind of humanness, but not to look on it as final.

If the sense of moral ambiguity discussed in the last chapter can be accepted, then the choice of finite and self-contained purpose is of that kind which is made in relation to authenticity and to nothing else. It chooses personal truth, the only available kind, and rejects the claims of the Law and the flesh. This it must do, but all those who do this do not see in it a finality. It may perhaps be the narrow way through to something further.

If there is, or could be, a way through we still have to realise that all the previous stages are necessary before it can be found or even sought. The stages of 'childhood' surrounded by the exterior wisdom of the Law are indispensable if the individual is to have sufficient confidence in himself to become aware of the demand of passion, whatever form it takes, and the years of tutelage will determine his ability to respond wholly to the demand when he hears it. The response to passion, which is just as essentially 'passionate', that is, 'spiritual' if it occurs by willed stages (as in successful dedication to an arranged marriage) and not in the strongly emotional version which makes it most obvious, begins to make it possible for the spirit to experience itself. From this grows the possibility of achieving personal authenticity and this must be done in relation to other people. But the growing 'spirituality' of a man makes him increasingly aware of what is still inauthentic in himself—that is, in his relations with others. And so, in the end, he realises a loneliness in which acts in relation to other people cannot any longer be a sufficient test of, or reason for, being. They are the only real things, and yet after all they are, as in the parable, 'dishonest'—not real. Their unreality makes demands which are a threat to personal reality. Human relationships have the right to make such demands and yet the response to them is a surrender to the inauthentic. In such a position the only safety, the only sense of reality as a human being, is experienced in the assertion of loneliness, as a deliberate act and not as something to be suffered.

All this is part of the necessary development towards maturity, but for many people it seems as if it must end there. The realisation of inability to communicate honestly feels like a repudiation of human relationships as a real part of being human, even when such relationships are still lived, and must be lived, as well as possible. And because it feels like a repudiation it is interpreted as a repudiation. In that case any way out of the accepted isolation feels like running away from the truth and must be resisted.

In practice this condition finds a way of tolerating itself by building deliberate artificial bridges between itself and other people. It creates responsibility and relationships out of its isolation, because it cannot accept that there can be prior responsibility or relationship (for what is prior to decision is not authentically human to this way of thinking). But, if one is not committed to claiming conscious self-creation in a void as the absolute of possible humanness, this doctrine of self-created responsibility—by which one's own actions are an implicit commitment of other people to similar actions—can be seen as a way of accepting the demands of human relationship as real in practice, while denying them in theory. It may be the attempt of the spirit (who is a Machiavellian sort of prince and will descend to any ruse that will serve his ends) to achieve by subterfuge what he cannot achieve by direct attack. The spirit, in its struggle to be itself, has to force the flesh to recognise not only itself as distinct, independent, but eventually to be prepared to abandon even that distinctness. For this distinctness, authentic as it may seem, is not the final wholeness of the spirit but the last, despairing defence of the flesh against annihilation. This, it seems to me, lies behind the fierce courage of much existentialist thinking. It is admirable, but it is incomplete, and its strength lies in its incompleteness. For the completion, if there be one, must lie in the dark regions below the conscious level, where the Law cannot reach and the devil is to be found.

It is comparatively easy to deal with the devil if you can comfort yourself with the idea that he is essentially something alien to yourself, a separate Being, with horns and a tail to show just how other he is. It is far more disturbing to realise that the devil who confronts us is part of ourselves, and the new dualism seems to be an attempt to assert his otherness, so that he can still be opposed as

6

alien. He may be part of ourselves but he is a sub-human part to be rejected and shut off as the price of true humanness. Medieval psychology saw it this way too. But if the devil in man is really part of human nature he can only be rejected at the cost of repudiating the possibility of being fully human. If I am not willing to accept a concept of humanness which rejects nine-tenths of human experience as non-human, that is, 'evil', then I must look honestly at the alternative. The alternative is to look for the significance as aspects of humanness of all human experience, making no *a priori* exclusion at all. The experience of what may be called the demonic must then be faced. The demonic, as far as it may be defined at this point, is the action of that area of human life which is beyond conscious control or intellectual apprehension, but which, when we oppose it, affects behaviour in unpredictable ways. Because of its 'unclubbable' quality the unconscious mind and the behaviour it motivates frightens us. It forces us to be aware of the regions we cannot reach, and the best defence against their incomprehensibility is to regard them as alien to ourselves, separate from ourselves, something we can and should oppose. This opposition may be necessary in order to preserve the structure of the Law. But it means that the evidences of the existence of the unreachable area of human nature are likely, when they do break through the opposition, to be violent, destructive and, in relation to the Law, 'evil'.

This area of human life must be faced because it is the narrow way which leads beyond the apparent impasse of a discontent which, present throughout history, has now become endemic to our society. Once we have realised ourselves as authentic individuals in the flesh this is the only way forward.

The world, the flesh and the devil are the traditional enemies of the spirit. Yet it seems that the spirit demands that we live not only in, but for, the world. We accept and use life in the flesh as the only means of liberating the spirit. And if we are to accept the implications of human life as we actually experience it, and try to find in that the material of its perfection, then we shall also have to find a way to get on with the devil in ourselves.

But 'the world' is human relations in so far as they manage to to get along without the spirit, therefore the release of the spirit means, eventually, the unnecessariness of the world. The flesh is human nature muddling along in its state of radical ignorance, therefore the flesh, too, ceases to be in proportion as its makeshifts are made unnecessary by the authenticity of the spirit. So perhaps the devil likewise is something we have to reckon with and work with, but which is temporary as a phenomenon of human life, whatever else he may be.

Neither the world nor the flesh are to be superseded by pretending that they don't exist, that they are not important, that we can safely outlaw them. Attempts to do any of these things can appear to succeed for a while but sooner or later the neglected aspect of ourselves gets its revenge, and its revenge is likely to take the form of the devil, because the devil is whatever we ourselves have made evil by opposing it, for however good a reason. The world and the flesh contain no devil as long as they are allowed to run things their own way. Rules that are merely practical and immediate, behaviour that is convenient and serviceable, are all ignorant of the devil, which is why for civilised societies and people he does not exist. But as soon as discontent forces people to search for a reality beyond or within convenience and order they meet the devil. They discover forces and impulses within themselves which do not fit in with the self-discovery within the framework of the Law. These impulses of man threaten his very existence as a being in the flesh and in the world—in which, as he knows very well, he has to live. These impulses are not 'sins' in the ordinary sense which I discussed in the introduction, but the sense of a power, a force.

Sometimes man threatened by such impulses can avoid the danger by compromise. He can give the devil his due by giving an outlet to motives and desires which, while not profitable to it, at least do not actually attack his existence in the world. In this way the devil can be kept comparatively harmless. The trouble about the devil, however, is that it is difficult to give him an inch without his taking an ell. Many are those who thought they could control him and exercise him and then stable him quietly, but found that he had the bit between his teeth and was heading back to the primeval wilderness from which he came. This experience is common enough. The outcome depends on the stage of spiritual development of the person concerned. In the early stages the discovery of the power of the devil seems so threatening to existence in the flesh that the fear of him is enough to bring about a complete return to the protection of the Law. Hence (until at least some sort of authentic passion succeeds in making a break) every influence that does not conform to the Law needs to be resisted, for the devil let loose in the nursery is capable of destroying not only the Law but also the flesh which the Law protects until from it and by it the spirit may grow. The devils of children are utterly terrifying and 'inhuman'. Stories like *The Turn of the Screw*, *High Wind in Jamaica* and *The Lord of the Flies* depend on this fact for the effect of horror they create. It is not until the Law has been outgrown (not abandoned) that the devil can be safely recognised for what he is.

The 'badness' of the devil at one stage consists in the fact that the flesh, without the Law, can only be chaotic, unorganised, producing jungle reactions which can prevent the communication of the spirit, the real self of a man. But once a human being in the flesh has been supported and developed by the Law and has then grown through the Law to authentic knowledge of himself as distinct, he needs to learn to let loose the power in himself 'in the spirit', including that power which is 'demonic'—that is, not tameable by the Law, and destructive of life in the flesh. So St Paul writes to the Corinthians with a mysterious command concerning an erring brother, telling them to 'hand him over to Satan for the destruction of the flesh'. Perhaps this is why great holiness and great wickedness are in some ways so similar in the fascination they exert and their power over other people, why both saints and lunatics occasionally have startling powers of mind reading and apparently of foretelling the future, and why 'wonders' appear to have been worked by people who are 'possessed' as well as by people of outstanding human goodness. (It is, of course, much easier to say that none of these peculiar things happen at all, but the evidence for them is enormous, and so varied in kind that it becomes very difficult to find methods of explaining them away.)

It is at least worth considering whether what we think of as demonic is not simply that aspect of human nature which cannot be organised by the Law to serve the needs of the world, so that it is a constant threat to both and constitutes their underlying weakness. Recent studies about schizophrenia seem to support this view. A recent and enthralling book, a personal account of what it feels like to be mad,[1] has an introduction by a psychiatrist in which the following passage occurs:

'In becoming aware of ourselves and others as persons we come to realise that we have to begin from a position wherein we are largely alienated from much experience. If we naively regard our norm of sanity as the measure of insanity then we are led to precisely the point of view that has been held until recently about schizophrenia, namely that it is an intrusion into a person's life of an essentially unintelligible organic process, of which the experience itself is a secondary consequence. But if we see our sanity as already a state of extreme alienation then we will be less ready to suppose that the schizophrenic is more alienated than we are from the totality of reality.'

Further on he says:

'. . . It is necessary to admit all domains of experience into our context of relevance if we are going to understand schizophrenia. Since natural science studies only the relation between things we are thus in a context of relevance that is without the domain of natural scientific investigation. We have to realise the phenomenal existence of an 'inner world' that goes beyond the realm of imagination, reveries, dreams, and even of unconscious phantasy. I can think of no better word for this experimental domain that lies 'beyond' the reach of perception,

[1] Morag Coate, *Beyond All reason*, Intr. R. D. Laing, M.B., Ch.B., D.P.M. (Constable), 1964.

thinking, dreams, phantasy, than the spiritual world—the domain of spirits, Powers, Thrones, Principalities, Seraphim, Cherubim, the Light . . . We are living in a different world in which, as Heidegger has put it, *the Dreadful has already happened*. The wholeness and holiness of Being is [in the schizophrenic] already split into the spiritual and the mundane' [whereas for the 'sane' the spiritual is simply covered over by the needs of the mundane—the region of the world and the flesh.]

This is the world in which, so Paul said, man's real struggle must take place. And it is a world in which it is easy to get lost if one ventures or is forced into it too soon. If this is so we are not entitled to deny the human relevance of the devil. The search for humanness, for the essential self, must finally come to 'realise' the devil, literally. It must recognise that he is real, and therefore of the whole. But if the region which he rules in us belongs to the whole human being it is not evil, for evil is that which prevents the discovery of the whole. Therefore it is no longer devilish when it is of the whole. But for as long as it is not realised as of the whole it is evil, and is the devil, and is extremely and pugnaciously and obtrusively real precisely as evil.

In this sense, then, it is true that the devil is evil and is real and utterly irredeemable. The devil remains the devil as long as he is separate, and opposed in separation. A notion of humanness that keeps man in the sphere of conscious individuality for ever must keep the devil, too, forever as the price of that individuality. So the spirit that claims human freedom in conscious decision alone finds itself finally enslaved, because it cannot do without the devil. To the world it is indifferent—it can serve it or not. It has dealt with the demands of the flesh (in so far as it is not shaped by the Law) by handing that over to the devil. And the devil, whose power is the power of the spirit, distorted by the demands of the flesh and untamed by the Law, is not slow to take advantage. Possibly this was the experience, at just this stage of development, which made Paul complain of 'an angel of Satan' which was sent to 'harass' him 'in the flesh'. He prayed to be delivered, but was told 'My grace is enough for you, my power is made perfect in weakness'.

So far, in our society, the Law has been strong enough to resist to some extent the pressure exerted by the devil. I wonder how long it can do so. This is too big a question to be usefully discussed in such general terms, but the fact remains that the future of the world (in both senses) depends ultimately on the psychological condition of human beings as such—on the degree of spiritual maturity reached by individual people.

The pursuit of maturity, at this point as at earlier ones, requires a symbol to focus its efforts, and the idea which is summed up in words like 'devil', 'Satan', 'evil', 'demonic' provides such a focus.

It is not for nothing that fairy tales of many countries tell of a final struggle in which the long-sought prince or princess can only be discovered in his or her true form after a prolonged fight in which the enemy is the beloved in some horrible form, sometimes a number of successive forms, each more terrifying than the last. And it is only when the terrible opponent has been finally killed that the true form appears, transformed and glorious. In some stories the opponent tries to disarm the hostility of the hero by taking a beautiful or pathetic form and appealing for mercy. But there must be no mercy, for behind the charm and fragility of the flesh is the untamed power of the devil. As for those who succumb to the deceptive beauty, or are vanquished by the dragon, they are turned to stone—petrified at this incomplete stage of development—or changed to wild beasts. This latter is a way of indicating the nature of the stage at which they are arrested, with the true self imprisoned and helpless in the world of appearances which it does not understand, a prey to its own jungle impulses and cut off from the community of the world and the protection of the Law by madness or something near it.

There are numberless variations on this theme, and all of them are interesting and significant. There is no need to expound them in detail because the varieties of the symbolic expression are only a clue to the variety encountered in actual experience. Everyone who has been through this kind of experience can recognise the relevance of the symbols—but only in retrospect, otherwise the struggle would not have the character of ignorance and fear and uncertainty which make it a real struggle. And of course those who do not come through are not aware of their true state but may explain it to themselves in whatever way makes it possible to live with it most easily.

The battle with the devil means, in unsymbolic terms, realising all that we know most clearly as 'devilish' as ineradicably part of ourselves, and knowing this not as a theory we subscribe to (which is easy, and makes one feel pleasantly superior and enlightened) but as a matter of profound personal experience. This is not something that one can achieve just by wanting to. It is something that happens as the natural development of the process of spiritual growth, but like all the 'happenings' of this process it is never and cannot be purely passive. It happens, but it is a happening that has to be voluntarily accepted, and it is this acceptance which is so hard that almost anything, even madness, can seem preferable. It is also not very common, or at least is not commonly recognised for what it is. Many arguments might be put forward to show that it is in fact 'normal', even though uncommon—among them the testimony of myths and fairytales. The only really convincing argument is personal experience, and that is naturally not communicable.

But there is a much more common experience which makes it easier to accept the idea of this assimilation and 'conversion' of the devil. If I am right in suggesting that the normal progress of a sexual relationship shows the basic pattern of human development on the way to freedom, and also helps to bring it about, then we should expect to discover the evidence of the devil in the sexual experience, and some indication of the necessity of his presence and activity.

One strong indication that sex is felt to be a main link with the demonic, and that this is a desirable thing, is to be found in many advertisements for books about sex, and for scents, clothes, cosmetics and so on, designed to attract the opposite sex. A common line in the copy is the suggestion that sex is 'wicked' and the assumption is that the idea of its wickedness will attract purchasers.

Among writers, Lawrence seems to have realised that sex provides an obvious channel of communication between the areas below and above the threshold of consciousness. But though Lawrence charted it he did not discover it. It seems likely that the recognition of the fact that sex does provide such a channel is the underlying reason for the fear and suspicion of sex not only in the Christian tradition but in many other systems that sought to develop the 'higher' powers of man. Once you have really opened up this channel anything can come out, therefore sex has always seemed something to be firmly and even fiercely controlled, and a fine mesh of conscious morality interposed through which the really destructive element may not pass.

Destructive of what? If I am right, destructive of the flesh. It is really quite reasonable to regard sex as peculiarly subject to 'evil' because it is indeed the area of living in which the devil has the best chance of making himself felt. It links conscious human activity with the primitive, the animal, the pre-conscious or 'natural' areas of human nature. What is let out when these elements come to the surface and make themselves felt as experience, consciously recognised and to be reckoned with, is immensely powerful and almost impossible to control. This is why it can be so frightening, so dangerous, this is why it can really be 'evil' not only in terms of the conditioned conscience but in reality, in that it can actually prevent the achievement of wholeness by, in a sense, 'exploding' and disintegrating the elements of a personality. When this happens the person can appear to 'run wild', to become reckless and desperate. But much more often he or she can become totally enslaved to whatever or whoever it was that provided the symbol by which the demonic power achieved release, be it a religious sect or an individual.

This is presumably the reason for the use of rites and symbols described by journalists as 'obscene' in many initiation rites. Mau Mau oath-taking ceremonies are an example that caught and intrigued the public imagination. Such things have been in some degree the condition of entry to almost all secret societies from the Hell-fire Club to College Fraternities and school gangs. The

7

performance of an action which is felt to be really 'evil'—that is, contrary to what is consciously accepted as right and good— forces the initiate to recognise the existence of evil in himself. He has done this thing, it is part of him, he can't escape it. By doing it he has lost his claim to the shelter of the Law which protects the kind of goodness he has hitherto known and which has supported and enfolded him. He is now isolated from it, he has therefore no alternative but to rely on the support of the 'evil' to which he has committed himself. But in this 'demonic' region his hitherto useful conscience is no use. Therefore he can only feel himself at all safe in it by obeying implicitly all the commands given in its name, and these commands may come from a real human being representing the group, or merely from within the mind of the person possessed. From now on, no other criterion of conduct is relevant in this area of living. But 'ordinary life' may be unaffected, which is why people are so surprised when an apparently—and really—'respectable' person is found to be addicted to devil-worshiper or is a murderer or a seducer of children. Only the need to feel 'at one' with the power to which one has committed oneself matters, for the alternative (even where no threat of physical death or torture is present) is isolation of a kind which human beings cannot bear.

But, if sex can be used to create a commitment to the devil that enslaves completely, it can also liberate the same demonic power in a form in which it can be used in the pursuit of wholeness. It is still dangerously powerful, it can still be misused because it *is* so powerful. But the danger of totally swamping the personality by this invasion from below need not be present. This particular danger occurs when the release of the demonic comes too soon. Possibly Lawrence thought that Connie's besotted state following the famous initiation into the demonic aspect of sex in *Lady Chatterley* was a good thing and proper to a woman in relation to a man. It seems to me that his observation was correct but his interpretation wrong. What seemed to him to be right and inevit- able in the development of the relationship was in fact a distortion of normality. Connie is not ready for this stage, she is not sufficiently developed as an individual in distinction to be able to 'take' such an initiation and grow by it to be *herself*. Therefore she does what immature personalities must do when exposed to the demonic—seek in it their whole existence and their only safety. Incidentally it seems to me that the debate about whether the famous episode in *Lady Chatterley* involves 'normal' or 'perverted' sex is quite beside the point, which is that Connie is made to feel that she had passed beyond the reach of ordinary values and the safety of the Law.

This has a special interest because, as David Holbrook shows very clearly in *The Quest for Love*, Lawrence's women, but especially Connie, are not like any real women except in moments of almost involuntary realism when the artist's fundamental honesty overcame the resistance of his personal emotional bias. Connie is really Lawrence's own feminine side, which he feared and must bully into total submission and passivity. The method he uses to bring this about is that of driving the immature personality beyond the safety of the Law so that it becomes totally dependent and 'will-less'—he hated a woman to will anything herself. It is particularly significant just because Lawrence did not fully realise what he was describing or its implications. There can be no love in Mellor's relationship with Connie—no tenderness or 'care'—because love would make her 'herself' and he cannot bear that she should be anything for 'her-self', but only 'his'. This is the effect intended by all 'initiations' of this type. They aim to produce will-less, conscience-less, in practice 'self-less' subjects of the one ruling authority, which may of course be a purely imaginary one. This 'self-less' state is the essence of the notion of demonic possession, when the personality is actually 'taken over' by the 'invasion from below'. In the gospels (especially Mark's) Christ is shown as victor over the demonic; therefore he cures the possessed, and in doing so he speaks to them in stern words which are a complete contrast to those he uses to the physically sick or even to sinners, with whom he is gentle and sympathetic. It is as if in cases of possession the 'real' person were, for the time being, 'not there' and so could not be addressed. We find the same

feeling expressed in *The Turn of the Screw*. The governess finds
that kindness and appeals and gestures of affection do not get
through to the children in the grip of their sinister friends. Only
violence does, but by then it is too late. Miles's 'self' is not
strong enough to save the life of his body, exhausted by tensions
and emotions too fierce for a child to cope with. But when Christ
has healed the possessed man at Gerasa we *then* find the patient
'sitting at his feet, clothed and in his right mind'. A relationship of
love is now possible, because the man is 'himself' again, to use the
significant phrase for one who has seemed to be 'absent', 'wander-
ing', 'out of his mind', or just 'not himself'. It is interesting, too,
that the healed man wants to stay with his healer, but Jesus sends
him home, to his own people, there to 'declare what God has
done for you'. He must be himself, he must grow up, now that love
has freed him.

The relation between what was once called possession and what
is now labelled psychic disorder is not clear and is a matter for
argument, though those who treat psychotics are less certain than
they used to be that they know exactly what is happening to their
patients. But whatever label we attach to this state, and whether or
not it reaches the dimensions of actual 'possession' or 'mental
illness', it is one in which the 'self' is clearly not in control or
able to communicate properly. Case histories show, over and over
again, lack of the security of love, and therefore inability to grow
up in love, as at least likely to change a tendency into an actual
psychosis. And in treatment much depends on the ability of the
doctor and nurses to 'get through' and inspire confidence in the
patient thus isolated. Before the self has discovered itself in the
security of being loved the demonic regions are dangerous, and
the sense of having lost contact with the parent system leaves the
personality at the mercy of the demonic. Objectively quite trivial
things can give the sense of loss of contact. Things done in initiation
rites, devil worship, and so on, sometimes seem to us ludicrous
rather than sinister. Children's gangs may ask their new members
to spit on a Church door, to take off their trousers, to recite an
obscene rhyme or something equally harmless. The significance

of these mildly silly kinds of behaviour is psychologically the same as the child-murder, Black Masses, or elaborate sexual orgies used by people with a larger 'normal' tolerance of behaviour. Such people needed something much more obviously and unmistakably 'evil' in order to achieve the same result. The result is the liberation of the personality from the Law. When it comes too early, it can only lead to enslavement to whatever provided the symbol of liberation, and this is a state very difficult to reverse.

So the protection from the demonic provided by Law, in Church or State or by public opinion, is necessary; yet people resent it. They may not know why, but the continuing fascination exerted by anything 'evil', and more especially by evil connected with sex, is a symptom of the fact that human beings cannot entirely rid themselves of the devil's insistent demand to be heard. In the first chapter I quoted, on this subject, a broadcast talk. The passage continues: 'In such things as these [the delight in cruelty, etc.] man is certainly not just a little lower than the angels, he is much lower than the animals; and to explain them only in terms of infantile trauma or social maladjustment does little justice to their radical character. *There is a residual element here which would appear to be characteristically human—or should one say satanic—rather than animal in origin.*' A fascination with ruins, darkness, bats, skulls, death, storms and the more unruly aspects of 'nature' was only one form of the revolt against the necessary Law, at a period when the overtly sexual could not comfortably be canvassed in public. Nowadays our newly emancipated younger generation revolt against the successful materialism of their parents and listen to the whispering of the devil in a more obvious, and probably safer place, for sex has a built-in humanness which was lacking in the symbols of release cultivated by the Romantic movement.

In spite of the obvious danger, sex is probably one of the best places in which to let loose the demonic, because sexual behaviour is not concerned *only* with the demonic side of human nature. It is concerned with a human relationship which is potentially a whole one. It has aspects which are animal, and it can include elements that relate people to the Law as well as elements that draw them away from it. But above all it is at least implicitly a loving relationship, and it is this fact which makes sex a hopeful setting for the encounter with the devil. In other words, the 'too soon' stage is any stage at which real love is not yet present. When people love each other they can, in time (perhaps very little time) achieve together a freedom from the Law, a liberation which sets them free into love. Together, and in the security of their together-ness, they can discover the unruly power within them, recognise its essential lawlessness, and yet not be frightened into submission to it. It can become part of their whole selves, and when that happens it is no longer a threat, it is no longer the enemy, the devil. As the Book of Revelation puts it, 'there shall no longer be anything accursed', because everything is theirs and of themselves. The loss of shame which, without love, can force people into the arms of the devil by cutting them off from the Law, becomes instead the way to real freedom. For shame is the necessary protection provided for the flesh by the Law. It is a good thing as long as it serves its proper purpose. But the freedom from shame which lovers sometimes discover is to them no danger but the supreme bond and power of their love.

The kind of recognition or knowledge of the demonic which makes it part of the human whole can only be the kind of 'know-ledge' which is contained in the New Testament use of the word. It means knowledge in love, the lucid, enlightened vision which goes with complete openness to the real self, the 'spirit' of Pauline psychology. And if sexual love is, as always, the type of this love it is not the only or even necessarily the best setting for the emancipation in love of the demonic aspect of life. The wholeness that can sometimes be clearly discerned in people who have chosen a life of virginity is evidence of this for those who are prepared to recognise it. The monastic vocation can truly be a journey to 'the wilder shores of love' for those with sufficient courage to venture there and encounter whatever dragons are to be found.

It is not for nothing that the Christian creed contains that odd phrase 'he descended into hell'. Whatever interpretation we put on it, it must mean that Christians have thought of Christ as putting himself in contact with the 'lower' world, with the 'evil' or at least unredeemed side of human nature. And it is significant that this event is related to his death, which Christian thought has always regarded as the final and complete expression of love for man. It is in the context of this love—the most complete kind of self-giving imaginable—that the Church thinks of Christ as 'descending into hell'. And it is after *this* that 'the third day he rose again'. The recognition and acceptance of the devil makes whole. He then ceases to be 'the devil', he is defeated, chained and cast out for ever.

It seems at least possible that the health and even survival of Western culture will depend on whether it can realise the devil. At the moment we seem to be far from doing so. On one side the forces of tradition and the Law still labour to suppress and contain him, and on the other the forces of 'progress' blithely proclaim that he doesn't exist, and that there is no danger or evil in those aspects of life which have traditionally been his territory. Meanwhile, the propagandists grow more skilful, the mental hospitals fill up and overflow, and politicians play at Tom Tiddler's ground.

A society is only as healthy as its members. As individuals we continue to be on one side attracted by the demonic and on the other side frightened of it to the point of pretending it doesn't exist.

On the whole, the medieval attitude was probably a safer one. People believed in a concrete and 'separate' devil, who was most certainly dangerous but who could be overcome. But the prevalence of heresies of an obviously demonic type, involving total loss of shame and an assurance of personal power and perfection amounting to godhead, show that it did not work altogether safely. In any case we can no longer tame the devil in this way. To give in to his fascination is not the way to freedom, neither is the sustained self-deception involved in denying him. Nietzsche, in the person of Zarathustra, saw the solution as killing and spewing out the serpent that threatened the life of the shepherd. But the laughter of the man who has done this is the laughter of the man who has cut himself off from love in his rejection of evil. He *will* not be whole because wholeness includes recognition of evil, and that is too humiliating for man in the pride of his achieved distinctness. We must find a way to realise the devil which will not destroy us, and the way is the way signified by the place of the demonic in sex. It is the way of love. We must have the apparently suicidal courage to swallow the serpent, so that, once eaten (and eating is always the sign of unity and love) he becomes part of ourselves.

The devil is a psychological fact. As such, Christians have to cope with him, and Christianity must include this inescapable element in human life in its design for freedom. It does, right from the beginning.

That strange episode known as the temptation of Christ is recorded by all three synoptic gospels (Mark in a very compressed form) which indicates that it had a special importance for the first generation of Christians. Its first significance for them was, of course, in relation to the messianic character of Jesus. But however the form of its presentation may have been influenced by this need to relate Christ to the prophesied Messiah, the narrative bears the signs of a personal experience.

It is common nowadays among Christians to suppose that the description of Satan as speaking and moving about is simply a vivid way of conveying to the disciples a purely 'spiritual' experience. It may be so but, if Aldous Huxley is right, the 'mind's antipodes', which easily become available to consciousness following the chemical changes induced by fasting, do typically contain such figures and adventures as are recorded in this narrative. Huxley suggests that what is seen in ways such as these appears 'good' or 'evil' according to the state of mind of the person at the time. 'Negative emotions' transform a 'heavenly' vision into a 'hellish' one. It is clear from the gospel narratives that Christ retired into the wilderness under the compulsion of a need to come to terms with the vocation made explicit to him at the time of his baptism. He had to face up to what it meant to him, a human being, to be 'the Son of God'. It was a time of stress, the flesh and the spirit were beginning the long struggle which reached a peak two or three years later in Gethsemane. So the visible and audible form of the struggle is perfectly understandable and natural in the circumstances. At the end of it 'angels came and ministered to him'. The peace of mind achieved at such cost changed the character of the vision from 'satanic' to 'angelic'.

The interesting thing about the accounts of the temptation is that it shows a stage at which the devil must be *consciously resisted*, for this resistance at this stage is the appropriate way towards ultimate freedom and wholeness. But the struggle in Gethsemane shows signs that by then the time had come to overcome the devil by complete acceptance of all that he could be and do, inwardly and outwardly.

The following is a very free paraphrase of the narrative in Matthew. It is designed solely to bring out the general human significance of the psychological situation:

Jesus was driven by the demands of the spirit to go into the wilderness where he had to undergo a struggle with evil. He fasted for a long time, and was very hungry. The temptation first took this form: the tempter said to him 'If you really are "a Son of God" (a man living by the spirit) then you have the right to do what you like with material things. They should be made to serve your needs, for you are their master. You could even turn these stones into bread.' (This intensely charged significance of ordinary things seen is, according to Huxley, characteristic of the visionary experience.) But Jesus answered, 'A man does not become whole by satisfying his material needs only. To force nature to serve me, which I could do, might even prevent me from getting the "food" of the whole man, which is knowledge in the spirit, the "word" that is the utterance in terms of the flesh of the deepest and unutterable reality for which we are searching. Even a little of this knowledge is worth any amount of material well-being.'

Then the devil took him to the Holy City (the exterior sign of all man's striving for freedom, embodied in an institution of 'the world'). And he put him on the highest point of the Temple, the centre and symbol of all man's hopes. And he said to him: 'If you are a Son of God, this great sign and hope is your natural possession. You can do what you like with it. Prove to yourself—and others—that you really are a man of the Spirit by demonstrating your power in this, your proper sphere.' But Jesus said: 'The power of the spirit is not something to be manipulated or exploited. If I did this it would show that I was not truly of the Spirit. The spirit must grow, not be forced.'

The devil took him to the top of a very high mountain. This signifies the highest solitary achievement of man in the flesh, the peak of distinctness. From there all the glory and achievements of man could be seen, spread out far below. And he said to him: 'If you will let me loose, so that I can permeate your whole personality, no human power or achievement will be beyond your reach. You will have no ruler or Law over you, everything will be at your feet.' Then Jesus said to him, '*Be gone*, Satan. The opening out to the spirit must only be made in love. It is only by *self-giving in love* that the real power and wholeness may be attained.' Then the devil left him, and angels came and ministered to him.

This strange story contains several of the elements of contemporary unease. There is the temptation to regard power over 'nature' as an end in itself, to which the objection (all too evident) is that by itself this does not satisfy the longing for wholeness, but can even prevent its pursuit. There is the temptation to feel that the discarding of religious superstition gives one the right to despise and crush the longing of which 'superstition' is the symptom and symbol. The answer to this is that it is not safe for even the most enlightened to play about with the forces represented by the thing we call religion.

And there is the temptation to feel that man, in his finally achieved pinnacle of self-consciousness, is at last his own master and can afford to regard the power in himself as obviously 'good' and to rule over and look down on all that is below the conscious level. The answer is that the end of this self-sufficiency without love (for love operates at least partly below the surface) is not wholeness but madness, and the power it gives is really the power of the devil whom we have chosen to call 'good' because we want him as an ally, but who is in reality still 'the devil'. At this stage he must be rejected and told 'be gone'. And he goes. But he comes back. We need to have him back, in the end. As Luke's gospel says, 'he departed from him until an opportune time'.

The 'opportune time' came when all that had been done and achieved in the power of the spirit was about to be undone and wasted; when isolation, not sought but imposed, was complete; when all the things on which people rely in order to 'do good' had failed, one after another. Personal qualities, ideals, hopes, human love, self-confidence, had fallen away. Even confidence in the power of the spirit had gone, or rather was rejected because it was no longer 'opportune'. Christ had apparently reached a stage where something radical had to happen to 'the spirit' in him, something which up to then had only been foreshadowed. 'This is your hour, and the power of darkness,' he told the guards sent to arrest him. 'The power of darkness' had to be overcome, no longer by rejection or resistance but by total acceptance, by 'swallowing the serpent'—alive, at that. It was an acceptance made out of love, otherwise it would not work, it would be not acceptance but capitulation to evil. But the condition of real acceptance is that it should be total, and that means that even though the motive is love the consciousness of that very motive must in the end be lost. Even the thing that makes sense of the whole ordeal finally goes. 'My God, my God, why hast thou forsaken me?'

CHAPTER VIII

'WAS IT NOT NECESSARY TO SUFFER THESE THINGS?'

Suffering and freedom

So far this study of the search for humanness has followed the spirit of man in its progress through its nursery stage in the flesh, undergoing education by the Law, achieving its breakthrough by passionate response in relation, discovering itself in the wider relation of a society, and faced with the need to release even those depths which, for long, it rightly regarded as evil and dangerous. Many of the stages on the way towards the fullness of being human are, as I noticed and as everyone knows, extremely painful. In this last chapter I shall ask why they are painful. Is there any reason for the fact that suffering is an inevitable part of human existence or is it evidence of the essential futility of being human? Over the path to wholeness hangs the huge cloud of pain, and beyond it is death. Suffering and death are the enemies and companions of man, twins whom he hates and cannot do without. There is no 'answer' to them in the sense of a hope of getting rid of them. If there is a way ahead it is not a way out but a way through.

But in seeking a way it is natural to want some kind of map to show that the effort is worthwhile, and a great deal has been written and said about 'the meaning of suffering'. A meaning is a pattern of ideas woven by the mind, a pattern whose parts are mentally linked in some way to individual facts of experience and observation. This linking system of fact to idea in the pattern, and idea to idea within the pattern, makes it possible to have consistent attitudes towards the facts of experience. Otherwise one could only react emotionally to separate experiences (mental or physical) and the resulting series of uncoordinated emotional responses would soon become intolerable.

The clearer and more coherent the design of the pattern, the easier it is for people to pass through experiences without too much emotional variation, hence the appeal of systems which present all aspects of life in clear-cut, easily identifiable relation to each other and demand as of necessity a particular type of reaction. This is probably a reason for the enduring influence of Thomism in the Catholic tradition.

It is at least arguable that such patterns of meaning are a protective device to enable the vulnerable personality to pass through certain stages of its development without serious damage. As such, they are justified, especially in relation to suffering, which is inevitable. A clear-cut meaning-pattern about suffering raises the ability to tolerate it above the level of most pains and griefs normally encountered, and makes it possible to carry on without the danger of being swamped by the emotional consequences of minor ills. In a paper to a conference of psychiatrists and others concerned with mental health, Doctor Victor Frankl recorded a personal experience in a concentration camp which is one of many examples of how a sense of meaning can make it possible to tolerate conditions of the deepest degradation and hopelessness. When he was taken to the camp he had to surrender, with his clothes, the manuscript of a book that represented his whole life's work, 'and I had to face the question whether this loss did not make my life void of meaning'. But the clothes he was then given were those of a Jewish gas-chamber victim, and in the pocket of these rags was a page of a Hebrew prayer book on which were lines of the Sh'ma Ysrohel—the command, 'thou shalt love the Lord thy God with all thy heart and with all thy soul and with all thy might'—or, as one might also interpret it, the command to say 'yes' to life despite whatever one has to face, be it suffering or even dying. 'A life, I told myself, whose meaning stands or falls on whether one can publish a manuscript ultimately would not be worth living'. Having lost one meaning he had to find another or perish.

But at a certain point in personal development the question arises, do these useful and necessary arrangements of ideas correspond to anything real in myself? Or are they merely an exterior protective garment, however useful?

One point to remember is that clothing, however clumsy and even ludicrous, has to be shaped in some sort of relation to the body that wears it. The relation may be arbitrary and uncomfortable, the cut and decoration of the garments may be influenced by ideas that bear no relation to the shape of the human figure, but at least it must be possible to wear them.

The same is true of meaning patterns. Those which are manifestly un-fitting for human beings are soon discarded, however attractive and impressive they may seem for a while. Sooner or later (the more peculiar the sooner) the facts of ordinary living will either modify the pattern or, if it is too rigid, force its abandonment. The history of Mormonism shows the former alternative, the latter has been demonstrated by the frequent ascetic millennial sects that grow up overnight and die down as quickly. The 'Exclusive' section of the Plymouth Brethren, whose doctrine is definitely Manichean in tendency, seem to be going their way to extinction for this latter reason.

If meaning-patterns that 'work' do so because they have some relation to the 'shape' of the human personality, it could be argued that there must be an ideal pattern that corresponds exactly to the reality of human nature. But meaning-patterns consist essentially of conscious ideas, and only a very small area of human life is conscious. Unconscious realities can only be represented in the pattern by symbols (as I suggested earlier in connection with symbols of 'wholeness' which focus the impulse of passion) and so we can never be directly aware of these realities in such a way as to represent them adequately in terms of the meaning-pattern. So although meaning-patterns are necessary for survival and growth they can never be more than clothing, representing in a more or less arbitrary fashion the shape of the person underneath.

But underneath the clothing is the naked body, and underneath the meaning-pattern is the real person. Clothing can help people to ignore or forget their naked selves for a long time. Some people never come to grips with the fact of their own unadorned physical self, and many more never come near to recognising a reality beneath the clothing of meaning-patterns under which they live so comfortably.

Meaning-patterns devised by men are no more a deception or a superfluity for developing human nature than clothes are. In a 'state of nature' we can do without both, weather permitting, but we have to emerge from that state of 'natural' indistinction, the oneness with the community which is that of the baby who has not yet discovered himself as an individual. Clothes not only keep us warm and dry but are a means of discovering and showing others who and what we are. In a unified community people wore the same sort of clothes nearly all the time, the style was virtually fixed by one's status in the community. The Renaissance explosion of individualism showed itself by, among other things, the rapidly changing fashions by which people can experiment with different ideas about themselves and their nature.

The changing meaning-patterns of history show exactly the same purpose and correspond startlingly to changes in dress. This is not really surprising, since both serve the same purpose, for clothes are the visible expression of part of the meaning-pattern shared by a particular community.

There is, on the other hand, another kind of pattern in human life which is simply the observed relation of actual events in life. This is how they, visibly, are; this is the order in which they occur; these are the results that follow from this. Such observations may be woven into a 'meaning-pattern' whose significance reaches beyond the events themselves, but the pattern of events is not of this kind, it simply is there. It may be that, in order to make use of this observed pattern we have to *treat* it as a meaning-pattern, but the thing itself simply is, independently of our meaning-interpretation. Of this kind is the pattern of a sexual relationship, of this kind also is the development of a child in relation to his parents. And because these things are simply human facts and not things we have invented, they are valid as tools to be used in evaluating other events in human life. If an event or a reaction has the same functional relationship to another event as we have observed in these fundamental human patterns, then we are justified in expecting a result which corresponds in terms of psychological realities to the result in the basic pattern.

If, then, it is right to be wary of asking too much of meaning-patterns in relation to suffering (though realising that they are invaluable for their proper purpose) it is not reasonable on this account to refuse to see any pattern at all when one is visibly there. Real patterns are not clear and satisfactory as meaning-patterns are. They are full of gaps and loose ends, they fade into uncertainty, they have no fixed and logical sequence worked out in self-contained continuity. This is inevitable because we are dealing with a reality which is very largely beyond our imaginative grasp. But the ignorance that surrounds the parts we can see is rather a guarantee of the reality of these parts than a reason for refusing to see anything at all.

The refusal to see any pattern is especially understandable in the face of human suffering. It is so manifestly futile, monstrous and purposeless, so unjust and arbitrary in its operation, so pervasive and yet so impossible to grasp, that the easiest, indeed the only possible reaction seems to be to shut out the consideration of it and to confine oneself to trying to relieve a little the very few examples of it that come within one's reach.

But this in itself shows an acknowledgement of some sort of pattern. It takes for granted that suffering is something that should be relieved, that the emotions that lead people to want to do so are basically desirable even if the motives may be mixed, and that the results of relieving suffering are so likely to be good that it is not normally necessary to debate seriously whether or not to try to relieve it. How far are these assumptions justified?

A woman who saw her baby being tortured would not stop to consider whether his suffering were a good or bad thing, she would just know that it was bad and must be prevented at all costs—even the cost of her own life. But such a woman can be conditioned by an imposed meaning-pattern to regard her child's suffering as not only inevitable but even good and beneficial. This is not a hypothetical example which has never happened. It happened in religions whose cult involved human, especially child, sacrifice, or practices of cultic mutilations. These things were regarded as an honour because they were essential to the welfare of the community. But it also happens now, when, for example, a painful operation is the only alternative to deformity or death. We regard mutilation as an act of worship to a god as monstrous, but accept the need for the same degree of suffering in the pursuit of health. The difference seems obvious to us, but the psychological modification required for the acceptance of such suffering is the same. The natural reaction has been modified to suit ends which normal emotions do not recognise.

It is therefore safe to assume that the basic human pattern of behaviour in relation to suffering involves a rejection of it as evil, to such an extent that it takes a very strong meaning-pattern to make it tolerable. Such a meaning-pattern protects the mother, in the example I chose, from the full normal impact of her baby's pain. But if a natural reaction must be forcibly modified for what seems a necessary purpose it means that the normal development of the personality is being arrested, at least for the time being. This is implicit in the idea that what happens *is* a 'modification', that is, a distortion (however beneficent) of normality. All religions or philosophies which aim at making it possible for people to tolerate suffering by keeping it 'outside' and interpreting it as somehow 'good' are therefore distorting the normal reaction, which is one of violent and unconditioned rejection of something inherently evil.

But there is another equally real part of the basic pattern of human development in relation to suffering. This is the fact that suffering, like passion, can create a channel of communication for the spirit. This is a fact and if the fact has been used too often to gloss over the evil of suffering, that is no excuse for pretending that it does not have such a power to open up the personality.

In order to understand why suffering has this power and yet more often serves rather to enclose and isolate than to set free it is necessary to glance back and see once more the relationship that has been explored in this book between the flesh and the spirit. Life in the flesh is life as we know it, 'nasty, brutish and short' maybe, but full of real if fleeting satisfactions and pleasures, and shot through with hopes and desires for something else. These desires fasten with irrational strength on to anything that will serve as a symbol for the elusive reality. The life of the flesh is the only life we can be sure of, it is therefore precious and worthy of care and respect. But the spirit is that which makes true man. It is a life which we know only through its manifestations in the restricting context of the flesh. The difference between behaviour according to the flesh and according to the spirit is a matter of ordinary experience, but there is no short-cut to the fullness of life in the spirit. It can only be reached by the use of the flesh. This is so much the case that anything that threatens to destroy the coherence of the flesh before it has had a chance to discover itself is a threat to the life of the spirit too. So the flesh protects itself from threatening destruction and it is necessary that it should do so. Of course 'the flesh' is not a person, making decisions. The word is merely a label for the complex of reactions which help people to adjust to the conditions of living. The mechanisms of defence against attack, of escape from the ever-present fear of aloneness, of compensation for weakness, are all what can legitimately be called stratagems of the flesh in its need to preserve itself from destruction.

On the other hand, the flesh must in the end be destroyed in the sense that the 'real' man cannot be one who is pushed around by these shifts and stratagems in order to survive in an alien environment. The life of the spirit finds nothing alien, is at one in itself and therefore with others, who are no longer a threat to the discovered self.

There is nothing new or unknown about this basic antithesis. The nature of the flesh and of its gradual transformation into the spirit are a matter of experience and a commonplace of modern psychology, though presented from various points of view and with various (sometimes contradictory) interpretations. The Christian terminology merely makes clear the purposefulness of the whole process, and presents the issues at stake not as a matter of social adjustment but of being fully human—or not.

Christianity has stressed the significance of suffering, and it is certainly true that a great deal of Christian writing and thinking about suffering has been morbid, and the 'monkish virtues' of 'celibacy, fasting, penance, mortification, self-denial, humility, silence, solitude,' which Hume placed firmly 'in the catalogue of vices', did not get there merely because the apostles of the Enlightenment were inclined to throw out the baby with the bath water. The cult of suffering, which plays so large a part in hagiography, can also have a thinly disguised sexual character which has been uncovered with much satisfaction by anti-Christian psychologists and their disciples. But it was not Freud but Paul who pointed out to the Church at Colossae that treating the body harshly was liable to be merely a way of consolidating the flesh. The Colossians were attracted by the doctrines that sought deliverance from the body, a purely 'spiritual' existence, by means of an elaborate ascesis: 'All these things are merely shadows, cast before; the solid reality is in Christ. So don't let people cut you off from that, persuading you to abase yourselves and worship elemental spirits, searching after visions, carried away by exalted emotions that have no basis in reason but only in the body; such things do not help you to live by the "head", the real master, from which the whole body, fed and co-ordinated throughout the whole system of joints and muscles, grows with a growth which is from God [i.e. proper to its real nature]. If, with Christ, you have died to the elemental spirits who rule the men in this world, why do you behave as if you still belonged to this world? Why do you submit to little rules?—"don't handle this, or eat that, or touch the other", all to do with things which in any case have only a fleeting importance, given them by human rules and teachings? Things of this kind can certainly seem to be vastly significant by promoting rigorous piety, self-abasement and severity to the body but they are really of no value in controlling the waywardness of the flesh.'

So much for the identification of Christianity with the cult of suffering. Even those saints in Christian history who were most renowned for their severity to their bodies became less so as they progressed in holiness and in true understanding of Christ's teaching. They often ceased to see any value in the rigorous self-torture in which they had indulged previously, and this not through any diminution in fervour but rather the opposite. Henry Suzo and Rose of Lima are two people devoted to terrifying penances who finally abandoned them.

This would not need saying if Christians had not themselves distorted the real Christian understanding of suffering by concentrating on the idea that the body itself was evil and 'the spirit' could only be released in proportion as the desires of the body were suppressed and rejected. The Pauline theology of the redemption needed only a little twist to make it support this view, but that little twist was one which altered the whole balance and made his humane and realistic psychology quite unrecognisable.

There are two facts about human beings and suffering, and they are both observable and capable of verification. One is the fact that suffering embitters and distorts people, making those who were happy and good malicious and cynical, or apathetic, withdrawn and sullenly resentful and hopeless.

The other is the fact that suffering brings out unguessed resources of heroism in the most unexpected people, and can release a radiance and whole-hearted warmth and even gaiety in quite atrocious circumstances. There is a light-heartedness that seems to be almost a normal accompaniment of martyrdom, and Thomas More joking on the scaffold is only one of many. It is only necessary to read the reports and memoirs of people who survived the Nazi concentration camps to find evidence of both these facts about the effects of suffering—the debasing of humanity and its exaltation. It seems that certain people, faced with appalling and hopeless pain, both physical and mental, become transformed—that is the only word for it—and the transformed self has the power to communicate an unutterable sense of joy and power that is almost irresistible. Other people in contact with this, themselves sunk in despair, feel it and may be drawn out of their hideous isolation to share something of this strong and vibrant life in the midst of death. And, reading descriptions of people who underwent this peculiar transformation, it is difficult not to realise that the characteristics of this state have no parallel in ordinary life except one. The quality of their intense liveness can only be compared to that of people transformed by passion. There is more than mere metaphor in the phrase common to so many martyrs, by which they described their approach to agony and death as going to meet their Bridegroom'.

This resemblance, which becomes more obvious the more one examines the two states, may be the clue to the appalling difference between the two kinds of reaction to suffering. The first is the reaction of the flesh, terrified of impending destruction, seeking any means to protect itself. The second is what happens when the spirit seizes its opportunity and, in the destruction of the flesh, comes into its own. Suffering, evil in itself, is a threat to the flesh but is not essentially dangerous to the spirit.

It is a cliché of romantic writing that real passion is as much painful as happy, and the more intense the emotion the less it can really be called pleasurable. Yet, however painful it is, no lover would willingly lose it in return for contentment and peace of mind. This seems very odd, yet is so common as to be taken for granted.

It seems that 'the spirit', the 'real' self, is all the time striving for self-discovery and the achievement of wholeness, the inner coherence and complete communication of the 'unleavened bread' without spaces of ignorance and fear and the phantoms that inhabit them. It is helpless in the flesh, but certain experiences of life in the flesh provide the conditions for the spirit to try to 'take over'. Sexual passion is such an opportunity, and once the life of the spirit has been given its chance by this or some other passion it grows stronger and can seize other opportunities to extend its conquest of the flesh—which nevertheless is never more than partial. The emotion of passion makes the initial conquest easy— but not, for all that, painless. The pain is the protest of the flesh at the destruction of its carefully devised network of adjustments to the conditions of life. Passion notoriously ignores and despises normal limitations—and the flesh suffers and dies, but only partly.

But when a person has learnt the lesson of passion, has refused to retreat into the protection of the flesh, but has tried to live as much as possible by the light that passion throws on the reality of human life and relationships, then the life of the spirit becomes strong enough to seize the opportunity offered by the fact that pain, physical or mental, is a threat to the life of the flesh. The danger to the flesh, a practical and real and obvious danger, is the chance for the spirit to invade the structure of the personality more and more completely. It is this invasion by the spirit that produces the extraordinary transformation that has often been observed. Those who lived to record their memories of Ann Franck's last days remembered the extraordinary radiance that she had, in the depths of humiliation and physical pain and degradation. Although she was so young she had grown, spiritually, very fast in those months of her family's strange confinement before they were finally arrested. It can even happen that the impact of suffering is the first big opportunity the spirit has had, and it acts with the full force of sudden passion. Ordinary goodness and contentment, or perhaps ordinary 'badness' and discontent, give way to a totally unexpected character. Nobody, least of all himself, had thought that Franz Jägerstätter had the makings of a martyr. A decent husband and father, he stood alone for the right of personal conscience to refuse military service in an unjust cause—the Nazi one. He accepted death with complete peacefulness and even joy when the time came. The agony of lonely decision was the spirit's opportunity. But this 'new' character is the real one, released in the destruction of the flesh. No pseudo-virtues, however useful and necessary, can stand up to acute suffering, which is why apparently admirable people sometimes 'go to pieces' in the face of really severe suffering. Their qualities were qualities of the flesh, they did not belong to the real self, the spirit.

But in order that the spirit may be able to seize its opportunity when it comes it is necessary, as I suggested earlier in this book (and indeed it is a commonplace of modern psychology that can also be confirmed by even the most casual observation) that the life of the flesh should itself have reached a certain stage of development. The flesh is the 'home' from which the journey begins, and it has to be a good home, a secure and loving home.

Every person has to learn himself in the flesh, and grow up in it by means of the Law before he is ready to be transformed in the spirit. It can happen at virtually any age, it can happen very fast, as in the case of Anne Frank, Elizabeth of Hungary and many other precocious heroes or heroines, but the stages of development can only be shortened and adapted, not dispensed with. On the other hand all sorts of different influences can prolong the stage of 'the Law' by which the flesh is protected and nourished, and this for the sake of the spirit whose development depends on it, since it must never be forgotten that flesh and spirit are not different things, or different stages of the same thing, but one is the reality of the other and, within the limits of our experience, neither can exist without the other.

While the flesh is not yet developed to the point at which it is capable of transformation by the spirit it must resist all attacks, and those things which are opportunities for the spirit at the right stage are dangerous to the point of being fatal if they come at the wrong stage. Therefore they must be avoided, dodged, changed into something else, passively resisted or actively attacked by any means that the individual temperament makes possible. But the flesh, being short-sighted and ignorant, cannot possibly tell when the time has come for it to make way, hence the sometimes frightful agonies (typically those of conversion, whether religious or anti-religious) that accompany any significant 'invasion' by the spirit, especially when this invasion has been unduly postponed or prevented by circumstances. The methods by which the flesh resists premature attacks are visible all round us and in ourselves, they are the stuff of which our elaborate and unsatisfactory 'normal relationships' are woven. Psychiatrists of various schools spend their lives trying to make clear to their patients just what particular stratagem each is employing in these attempts to preserve the integrity of the flesh. Each case in their reports is one more example of this attempt to avoid the attacks of the spirit. The purpose of the help and treatment given in this context is to complete, deliberately and 'artificially', the development of the flesh which has somehow been prevented from taking place 'naturally', so that, when the flesh has finished 'growing up', it can begin to respond to the demands of the spirit.

In many cases it can only be done by means of such artificial help, but experience shows that it does occur spontaneously and this spontaneous occurrence makes the plots of many of the great stories of passion and heroism, both fictional and 'true'. (But both are true, and the fictional ones may be 'truer' in the sense that they can convey the reality more certainly and immediately to the listening heart.) What artificial help is doing is not, as some people seem to fear, to create a new temperament, or superimpose artificial qualities on existing ones, but merely to assist the natural development by artificial means, in the same way that surgical or orthopaedic treatment for a deformed child is intended to help the body to achieve something as near as possible to the natural condition which has been prevented by the effects of some external influence (even a prenatal one). This is a process of assisting growth, not of making growth unnecessary. But only the child's own will and desire can then enable him to *use* the physical power that has been restored to him. So also the spirit of a man is himself, and only he can say yes or no to the demands it makes.

For even when the right point of development has been reached the flesh still cries out against destruction. It is so beautiful and so worthwhile and yet its destruction is the condition of real living.

That is the agony and the paradox behind the problem of suffering. It is the same for everyone and there are only two choices—to cling to the flesh no matter what the cost, or to follow the demands of the spirit, no matter what the cost. And the cost is high, in both cases, for in the end no man can serve two masters. All that Christianity does is to make it clear precisely what the choice entails, so that no room is left for persuading oneself that the needs of the flesh are, for all their reasonableness, the demands of the real self. The white light of Christ on this choice does not make it any easier. On the contrary, the clearer the realisation of what is at stake the more terrible the choice appears, for it is clear beyond evasion that response to the spirit means to be at least willing to abandon all that is sweet and comforting and good about life in the flesh, wherever it conflicts with the demands of the spirit.

It can sound dramatic and unreal, put like this, and yet this choice is a matter of everyday experience, in little ways and big ones, although the explicit and final choice is comparatively rare. But the naked presentation of what is entailed in this choice when it is pushed to its logical and furthest extreme shows up the meaning of the little daily choices between the flesh and the spirit, between openness and defensive isolation, between love and selfishness, and this is precisely the significance of the passion of Christ in Christian thought. It is not because suffering has some mysterious value of its own that Christians, from the first generation onwards, have emphasised the importance of the last few hours of the life of their founder. It is simply that his death shows a human being prepared to complete the choice of the spirit down to the last unutterable detail, even to death. All the things that the flesh shrinks from—and rightly—are here accepted as opportunities for the take-over by the spirit. This is not merely the big, dramatic, and therefore rather satisfying courage and endurance of the myth —hero, but something much nearer and more excruciatingly familiar in our own experience. Physical pain is bearable if there is a strong enough motive to uphold courage, a purpose which the pain is serving whether it be as witness to a great truth or as a means to regain health. The sense of futility, the conviction of failure, the experience of helplessness, ridicule, minor teasing and embarrassment and major humiliation and personal outrage— these are the things one dreads far more than physical pain or even profound grief. When all these, pushed to extremes, are combined with the sense of human betrayal and isolation and the overwhelming reality of excruciating physical torture, this seems indeed the destruction of all that we mean by the flesh.

But the last stronghold of the flesh is precisely the point at which flesh and spirit are virtually one, the point at which the spirit makes its demand and the flesh yields, the point at which the desire for wholeness, for 'salvation' thrusts into the unknown. As long as this ultimate point is still aware of itself, still asserting its identity against all that the forces of destruction can do, so long is the flesh still present.

Faced with this final defence, it is impossible not to wonder about the difference in the mind of Christ between what he called 'God' and what he called 'My Father'. It is tempting, and curiously enlightening, to notice that the final agony of the flesh, the conquest of this ultimate stronghold of personal awareness, is signified by a quotation from the psalms—an appeal to the God of the old covenant, who has 'forsaken' him and whose loss he must accept. This is the final loss of all that could support the life of the flesh, and after this, indeed, 'it is finished'. But the conclusion is not here, for the last words of Christ were not the announcement of the end of the flesh but the heralding of a new state: 'Father, into your hands I give my spirit.' The real self, the spirit, has taken over, has discovered itself at last. 'Father'—the origin, the basic reality, the whole from which the individual has gradually distinguished himself, until he has reached a stage at which he can return to that wholeness, not with the helpless indistinction of the baby but with the willed and deliberate self-giving of the fully conscious adult. This is the reality of love, this is the final reality of being human.

Is appalling suffering really the price that must be paid for life in the spirit? And if so, is it worth it, since life in the flesh is the only one of which we can be certain?

First of all, from all that has been gathered in the analysis of suffering in this chapter, it seems clear that suffering is only accidentally the means for the liberation of the spirit. It is so because in the fairly successful attempts of human beings through the ages to adjust themselves to their environment and to each other it is natural that all the pleasant, comforting aspects of being alive should form the mainstay of 'life in the flesh', giving point to existence and making the unpleasant things more bearable. So 'life in the flesh' includes all that is lovely and satisfying and pleasurable and beautiful in any way. And all this goodness is 'real' goodness—that is, we know it as good because we recognise that somehow it corresponds to the truth of the 'real self' that makes a human being human. We don't want to lose these things, and we are right, because they are good. And yet they are inextricably part of 'life in the flesh', and the spirit must overcome not merely the obviously restricting and inadequate and 'bad' aspects of life in the flesh but also those lovely things which actually hold it together and make it liveable. There is no alternative, because the web is so close that the lovely and honest cannot be separated from the ugly and dishonest without destroying the whole. This destroying is what, in Pauline psychology, the 'death' of the Christian (and, first, of Christ) means. Suffering is 'accidental', but inevitable in the circumstances. The author of the Letter to the Jewish Christians makes the point in a way rather different from Paul's when he writes: 'When he was in the flesh he prayed and implored, with strong outcry and tears, the one who could save him from death' (it is interesting to see, here again, the old covenant idea of God presented as being for the defence of the flesh) 'and he was heard, because of his piety [this seems to mean that his acceptance—this is the implication of the word translated 'piety' or 'reverence'—won deliverance not from physical death, which it obviously did not, but from the thing in death that the flesh fears] but although he was already "the Son" he achieved perfection [wholeness] by learning obedience [complete "openness"] through the things which he suffered, and was able to communicate that salvation to all who are willing to accept it from him.'

If suffering of some kind is inevitable if the spirit is to achieve the transformation of life in the flesh, is it worth it?

Even if the development towards maturity which I have sketched in this book is accepted as more or less valid, it still does not follow that it must be traced through to its logical end. It may be suggested that since the means are certainly painful, and the end uncertain, it is wiser to try to arrest the process at some convenient point. The question then remains, how is this to be done and, if it is done, what is going to happen to the great prince who is still in prison, though allowed out in disguise like the Black Bull of Norway, or in the obscurity of disguising night, like Cupid? Sooner or later, it seems likely that Psyche will want to find out what he really looks like. Perhaps it is better for her to be forced to contain her curiosity.

But the Christian will answer that Psyche's restless desire to see clearly is justified, that the price that must be paid is not too high. He affirms that, although we have no direct experience of its completeness, we have experience of a reality sufficiently clear in its incompleteness to justify us in taking Christ's word for it that such completeness is attainable, since he attained it. What that completeness is, when actually lived, we cannot possibly know, and Christ's communication of it to his followers was, inevitably, intellectually ambiguous. It could only express itself in terms of the ideas by which their minds were accustomed to deal with facts. It is enough to say that whatever it was it carried complete conviction, and that conviction caused, within weeks, an explosion of passion and power that changed the course of history.

To go further than that would not be helpful, since the fact of what the first Christians did is not seriously in dispute, whereas the reason why they did it is. But whether one accepts Christ's claim or whether one rejects it the choice that he had to make has still to be made, and it is made, as he made it, alone.

But while it is being made—and although the final expression of it may be sudden, dateable and crucial, that ultimate decision is prepared through many years of struggle and uncertainty and effort at authentic choice—the personal attitude to personal suffering must also and at the same time grapple with the huge and paralysing fact of other people's suffering, of the futile, disgusting mess of human life, of destruction and fear and misery and muddle, the pain of the innocent and the hatred of the guilty.

Suffering is evil, it should not *be*: this is one thing we are certain of. It can ennoble, more often it degrades. It should be overcome, yet without it there would be no effort, no forward movement, no humanness. We are caught again in the queer, inverted morality that Christ recognised so clearly. He laboured tirelessly to relieve suffering and yet was constantly aware that it must be that evil should come. The awful sense of helplessness and horror in the face of the magnitude of human misery was no novelty to him.

Like every man who suffers the agony of compassion he was oppressed by the hugeness of the need and the ridiculous inadequacy of one person's ability to meet it, however much a 'Son of God' that person might be. He was aware, too, that even when he could bring relief he was only touching the surface of the problem, hence the gospels' constant coupling of 'change of heart' with physical healing, demanding the former sometimes as a condition, sometimes in consequence, of the latter. In the gospel accounts of healing there is a curious atmosphere of almost desperate resignation, as if Christ were prepared to work himself to exhaustion in order to help the people who demanded his love, but was haunted by the obvious fact that he was not really making contact with them at all. The fact that he had not achieved any kind of real communication with the vast majority was all too apparent later. But he went on healing.

This is probably the only thing to do. To refuse to do anything because one cannot do all is to contradict the fundamental human knowledge that evil is evil and must be resisted at all costs. But whatever is done can only be done 'in the flesh' with all the limitations of effectiveness or even of purpose that that involves. There may, from time to time, be a real contact 'in the spirit' by means of the gesture of compassion; occasionally it brings a moment of truth, of 'honesty' between people. Mostly we have to accept the fact that all we do is 'dishonest' at best. We have to put up with the fact that there are no short-cuts, and that the only way to communication in the spirit (the desire for which is the reason for our innate conviction that suffering, which cuts people off from each other, is evil) is by way of the misleading, ridiculously inadequate and unsatisfactory means available to the flesh. It involves accepting the utter unreasonableness and morally nauseating character of all suffering, because if I get angry about it I know that probably I am only trying to ward off its possible threat to myself in the flesh. And yet I must be angry because real anger that comes from the heart is another form of compassion. Can one both accept and be angry? This is what Christ did, and the combination, odd as it seems, is characteristic of what St Paul called 'charity'. 'Love' is not really the best word for it because love is, as nearly as one can define it, the 'spirit' of a person in its activity. 'Charity' is the way in which this activity manifests and discovers itself, whereas 'passion' is the means, the 'channel', by which love (which is of the spirit) in its various forms is able to seize power over some area of the flesh and transform it. The passage in which Paul tried to explain to his bewildered Corinthian converts what kind of activity really expressed the nature of life in the spirit is probably the most famous in Christian literature. This is Paul's idea about how a human being should behave, in his condition as he is, inescapably in the flesh, but striving to discover the reality which is life in the spirit. It has to do with the themes that form the core of this book—the desire for real knowledge with the 'openness' which is created by passion, the luminous reasonableness of the perfectly irrational compromise which is upside-down morality, the humility of accepted ignorance, and the curiosity of the seeker. It has to do with the necessity of the flesh, and its final futility, with acceptance of the world, and breaking through it.

So this book is perhaps merely an introduction and a fanfare for St Paul. He wrote about the true ways of love expressed in charity to his tiresome converts at Corinth who were so thrilled with their exciting gifts and offices and their own great importance that they were in danger of developing a spiritual squint.

And if I have taken his words and recast them into a form that links them more clearly with the themes of this book I think Paul, who was always ready to be all things to all men, would understand.

If I speak any number of languages and can expound all kinds of esoteric learning in ways which mean nothing to ordinary people, I shall communicate about as effectively as the noisy reverberations of gongs or cymbals, so long as I speak without charity. I may have occult gifts, I may have profound insight into human life, I may be deeply learned in all the sciences, I may have such a grasp of the deepest mysteries that no wonder seems beyond me, but if I have these undirected by charity they are worthless in terms of real human development. I can make heroic gestures, distributing all my worldly goods, I can even be prepared to die for a worthy cause, but it will be purely for my own glory if I do it without charity, and so all this is to no purpose.

Charity accepts the fact that there are no short cuts to human perfection, either in time or in people—who cannot be forced and must be gently treated. Charity is not interested in 'I' and therefore does not suffer from jealousy or feel the need to show off, to despise or snub other people in order to feel important. The charitable person does not get irritated or resentful because he does not need to protect himself from others, and for the same reason he feels no satisfaction over tales of other people's misdeeds, but takes an unaffected pleasure in everything that is true and real, whatever its source. Because charity involves openness to what is real, and is undeterred by superficial qualities, it is prepared to put up with anything in the service of that reality. It will not cease to recognise the true person under the distracting appearances, and therefore to trust in that truth, and to endure whatever is necessary for its sake.

For charity does not have a limited function, as other human gifts do. The techniques used to inspire and encourage people are necessary when charity is insufficient. Languages and sciences must all be outgrown eventually, for our most expert science can only be partial, our most profound insights are at best inadequate, so that perfect understanding will naturally make them superfluous. In the same way, when I was a child I used childish words, my thoughts and reasons were those which a child can grasp, but since I have grown up I no longer find them relevant. The human condition as we know it gives us knowledge which is like a dim reflection of the real thing, but we are destined to see things as they are. In life as we experience it knowledge is bound to be a mere fraction of reality, but what we shall finally experience is un-hampered communication, knowing and being known, perfectly.

But meanwhile at least we have three things to help us, which will not let us down. They are faith (which seeks wholeness and freedom) and hope (which assures us that the search is worth pursuing) and charity (which is the means whereby we both search and find). So, finally, they are all summed up by charity.